9/11

THE
SIMPLE
FACTS

WHY THE OFFICIAL STORY
CAN'T POSSIBLY BE TRUE

ARTHUR NAIMAN

WITH GREGG ROBERTS &
AE911 TRUTH FOR WTC TECHNICAL HELP

THE REAL STORY SERIES

PUBLISHED BY SOFT SKULL PRESS

THIS BOOK IS DEDICATED TO THE THOUSANDS OF
9/11 TRUTH RESEARCHERS AND ACTIVISTS—
ESPECIALLY UNSUNG ONES, LIKE J.T. WALDRON—
WHO HAVE KEPT THIS ISSUE ALIVE AND
IN FRONT OF THE PUBLIC FOR TEN YEARS.
THEY'VE PATIENTLY BATHED SKEPTICS LIKE ME
IN THE BRIGHT LIGHT OF REASON
UNTIL WE FINALLY OPENED OUR EYES.
PATIENCE IS NOT A VIRTUE
I'M WELL ACQUAINTED WITH,
SO I'M PARTICULARLY IMPRESSED BY
THEIR SEEMINGLY ENDLESS SUPPLIES OF IT.

Inside design, layout and text, copy-editing, proofreading, tinyURL creation, link-checking, photo research, cover design, layout and copy: Arthur Naiman

Research, contributions, fact-checking, copy-editing, link-checking and proofreading: Gregg Roberts

World Trade Center technical assistance: AE911Truth

Final link-checking and proofreading: Kimberly Ehart

Index: Ty Koontz   *Logistical support:* Karen Bodding

Cover photo: **Gulnara Samoilova** (gulnarasamoilova.com)

Graphics enhancement: Lyon Leifer

Production coordinator: Julie Pinkerton

Series editor: Arthur Naiman

Fonts: Bookman (text), Optima (notes, etc.), LIBERTY (headers), **LITHOS BLACK** (front cover, etc.) **Gill Sans Bold** (back cover)

THE REAL STORY SERIES
IS PUBLISHED BY SOFT SKULL PRESS AND
DISTRIBUTED BY PUBLISHERS GROUP WEST

TABLE OF CONTENTS

Introduction

At some level of the government, at some point in time...there was an agreement not to tell the truth about what happened.*

John Farmer, Senior Counsel to the 9/11 Commission

The events of September 11, 2001 were, to put it mildly, major crimes that need to be investigated. But people who question the official story tend to get dismissed as "conspiracy theorists." To try to prevent this book from being dumped into that category, I've ignored theories about who did what and have focused on simply showing the flaws in the official version of events and pointing out the endless number of obvious facts it can't explain.

Before I dive into that, however, let's take a brief moment to consider the phrase *conspiracy theory*. The world is full of scary stuff, and the more you know, the scarier it can get. When knowledge leads to terrifying conclusions, people look for ways not to pay attention to it. Calling a clearly reasoned, evidence-based argument a "conspiracy theory" fits that purpose admirably. Once you slap that label on it, you're free to ignore it.

As for the *literal* meaning of the phrase, consider the official version of events: A bunch of Islamic fundamentalists, mostly

---

* *St. Louis Post-Dispatch*, 9/6/09, http://tinyurl.com/farmersquote

Saudis, acting under the direction of Osama bin Laden and other leaders of al-Qaeda, conspired to kill large numbers of Americans—and succeeded in doing so—by hijacking commercial airliners and flying them into US buildings. Whatever parts of that story are or aren't true, if *that* doesn't qualify as a conspiracy theory, it's hard to know what would. But it doesn't get *called* a conspiracy theory because that phrase is reserved for ideas you want to *discount.*

In a (probably fruitless) attempt to avoid that label, this book will restrict itself to the hard evidence that's led more than 1500 architects and engineers (with more than 25,000 years of professional experience), as well as thousands of senior government, military, CIA and FBI officials, pilots and other aviation professionals, firefighters, 9/11 family members and survivors, scholars, medical professionals, broadcasters, reporters, authors, publishers, actors, directors and musicians, many of whom you'll recognize—plus tens of thousands of ordinary citizens you won't—to call for a new, thorough, independent investigation.*

All I ask is that you, like them, actually *look at the evidence.* So here it is.

---

* http://www.patriotsquestion911.com (We can't vouch for the accuracy of every one of the thousands of listings on this site, but since it gives citations for all of its quotes, you can check things out for yourself.) There are two other lists—of building professionals and the general public—at http://ae911truth.org .

The official story, and why it can't be true

Buildings can be destroyed by a number of different forces, each of which has very different characteristics. By identifying those characteristics, you can determine what caused the destruction—or at least rule out some impossible candidates. That's exactly what several government agencies were charged with doing with regard to the World Trade Center attacks.

Similar investigations, such as the ones that looked into Pearl Harbor, the JFK assassination and the space shuttle disasters, all started within about a week. Yet the Bush Administration and Congress refused to open a comprehensive, high-level investigation of 9/11 for 441 days, relenting only after intensive demands by relatives of the victims.

Five investigations took place in all and they each had serious problems (failure to consider relevant evidence, conflicts of interest, allowing witnesses not to cooperate, and so on). The first two reports were issued in 2002: one jointly issued by the House Permanent Select Committee on Intelligence and the Senate Select Committee on Intelligence, and another from FEMA (the Federal Emergency Management Agency, which did such a wonderful job on Hurricane Katrina).

Funding for the FEMA investigation was only $600,000 and it appears that not a penny of that measly sum went to engineers actually analyzing data (they all worked as volunteers). Not surprisingly, *Fire Engineering* magazine called the report "a half-baked farce."*

FEMA came up with what came to be called the "pancake" theory, which basically proposed that the Twin Towers' floor trusses sagged due to fire, which caused the bolts that attached them to the perimeter columns to break free, which caused adjacent floor trusses to pull away in a chain reaction that "zippered" around the building. That caused the floors to fall, smashing down one on top of the other, all the way to the ground.

But if the *bolts* had failed, that would have been the fault of the building's designers, engineers or suppliers, not the terrorists, and real-estate investor Larry Silverstein, who'd just secured a 99-year lease on the complex in late July 2001, wouldn't have been able to collect on the multi-billion-dollar anti-terrorism insurance policy he'd taken out immediately after signing the lease.

So he responded by funding his own private investigation, using the NYC-based engineering firm of Weidlinger Associates. The resulting Silverstein/Weidlinger report concluded that the bolts held tight—so much so, in fact, that the sagging floors

---

* Bill Manning, "$elling out the Investigation," *Fire Engineering*, 1/1/02, http://tinyurl.com/manningarticle (For a brief critique of the FEMA report, see http://tinyurl.com/FEMAinvestigation .)

pulled the external columns inward and "the failure of columns alone, independent of the floors, explains the collapses." Since the bolts didn't fail, the terrorists *were* at fault and Silverstein and his associates would get their money.*

Then came the 9/11 Commission, which issued its report in 2004. Although it was supposed to be a high-level, comprehensive investigation, it conducted no criminal inquiries. It had no subpoena power, no special prosecutor, few open public meetings and virtually no scientific presentations.

Its report was criticized by its own co-chairs, by more than half the commissioners overall, by several members of Congress and by dozens of former members of the national security establishment.

Senior 9/11 Commission Counsel John Farmer told the *Washington Post* that "we were shocked at how different the truth was from the way it was described." He also claimed that the commission's executive director, Philip Zelikow, sent a small group of insiders a secret document outlining the commission's *predetermined* conclusions.

Commissioner Tim Roemer told CNN that "we were extremely frustrated with the false

---

* Kevin Ryan, "9/11: Looking for Truth in Credentials:
   The Peculiar WTC 'Experts,'" *Global Research,* 3/13/07,
                                     http://tinyurl.com/kevinryan1

statements we were getting." And before resigning in disgust, Commissioner (and former US Senator) Max Cleland stated that "the investigation is...a national scandal."*

Amazingly, the 9/11 Commission's report didn't even *mention* World Trade Center 7, a 47-story skyscraper that would have been the tallest building in 33 states and whose complete, precipitous, straight-down collapse—and "evaporated" steel—baffled engineers.[†]

Given all the criticisms of, defections from, and obvious omissions in the 9/11 Commission's report (and the growing momentum of the 9/11 truth movement), the government clearly needed something more comprehensive and convincing. Fortunately, they had another report in the works. Since the 2002 FEMA debacle, the National Institute of Standards and Technology (NIST) had been working on a report of their own, for which Congress had given them a budget of twenty million dollars.

NIST's original findings, first reported in their "final" draft report of October 2004, consisted of considerably different stories for the

* http://tinyurl.com/commission1 provides an overview of the 9/11 Commission's conflicts of interest. For more info, go to http://tinyurl.com/commission2 .

† James Glanz, "Engineers are baffled over the collapse of 7 WTC; steel members have been partly evaporated," *New York Times,* 11/29/01

two Twin Towers.* But NIST modified that nine months later in their "final, final" report, attributing the collapse of both buildings to Silverstein's column-failure theory, with no mention of pancaking.†

The report was a classic TNRAT ("they'll never read all this")—a 10,000-page mountain of mostly irrelevant documentation that did not, for all its length, "actually include the structural behavior...after the conditions for collapse initiation were reached."§

It's not that that's hard to do: for *no* money, two independent researchers produced code that does those calculations in real-time on a typical home PC.** NIST, however, merely stated, with no engineering analysis whatsoever, that "the structure below the level of collapse initiation offered minimal resistance to the falling building mass at and above the impact zone."††

When victim family members Bob McIlvaine and Bob Doyle, architect Richard Gage, physicist Steven Jones, and chemists Kevin Ryan and Frank Legge inquired about this amazing

---

* NIST, NCSTAR 1 draft, p. xliii, fn. 2,
                                    http://tinyurl.com/NISTexec
† http://wtc.nist.gov/NCSTAR1

§ http://tinyurl.com/NISTresponse

** http://tinyurl.com/grazkeeling ;
                                http://tinyurl.com/collapsemodel

††NIST, NCSTAR 1, §6.14.4, http://tinyurl.com/NISTsFAQ and
                                http://tinyurl.com/FAQreply

omission, NIST responded, "We are unable to provide a full explanation of the total collapse [of the Twin Towers]"—even though that was precisely their job! Oh well—another twenty million of our tax dollars down the drain.*

As part of their investigation, NIST hired Underwriters Laboratories to build floor trusses like the ones in the Twin Towers, subject them to fires much hotter than any in the towers could have been, and then pile on twice as much weight as the actual trusses in the towers bore. In spite of these rigorous tests, *none of the trusses failed.* The maximum amount of sag UL was able to produce was three inches.

NIST's response? They threw out the UL data and claimed that, according to their computer *simulations*, the trusses in the towers *should have* sagged 42 inches—*fourteen times more than UL's actual physical tests had shown!†*

When Kevin Ryan of Underwriter Labs wrote NIST a public letter stating that "the results of [UL's] tests showed that [the Twin

---

* http://tinyurl.com/NISTcant

† According to http://tinyurl.com/kevinryan2, note 14, "The extent of the floor deck sagging after the unrealistic time of two hours can be seen in NCSTAR 1-6, fig. 3-11 (p. 49). The three-inch result is visible there or, based on the 45-minute duration of fires in the failure zones, it can be seen in the graph in fig. 3-15 (p. 52). The computer result of 42 inches of sagging is noted in the same report, chap. 9, fig. 9-6 (p. 297)." Http://tinyurl.com/hoffmanryan gives *54 inches* as the computer-predicted amount of sag—*eighteen times the actual physical result!*

Towers] should have easily withstood the thermal stress caused by burning jet fuel [and office materials]," he was fired from his job.*

(NIST's first report didn't discuss Building 7 either; it was covered in a separate report that didn't come out until 2008. I'll discuss it in the chapter on Building 7.)

For more details on the failings of NIST's 2005 report on the Twin Towers—its startling omissions and fudged data—see Jim Hoffman's *Building a Better Mirage.*†

There are so many things wrong with these varying versions of events that it's hard to know where to begin. I'll come at them one step at a time, piling unlikelihood upon impossibility, so you'll get a full appreciation of how bizarre, strained and nonsensical they are. You won't need an advanced degree to follow any of this—just a little common sense.

All the official explanations have one basic idea in common: *the impact of the planes and the fires they caused weakened the Twin Towers to the point where gravity pulled them down.* There's only one problem with that basic idea: it can't account for any of the easily observable facts.

---

* http://tinyurl.com/ryanfired ; http://tinyurl.com/ultestingryan ;
                              http://tinyurl.com/ryanfired2

† http://tinyurl.com/bettermirage ;
                              http://tinyurl.com/collapsetheories

Certain events are pretty much undisputed: At 8:47 am on September 11, 2001, American Airlines Flight 11 crashed into WTC 1 (World Trade Center One—the North Tower), creating an impact hole that extended six floors, from the 93rd through the 98th.* At 9:03 am, United Airlines Flight 175 crashed into WTC 2 (World Trade Center Two—the South Tower), creating an impact hole that extended seven floors, from the 78th through the 84th.†

In both cases there was a large initial fireball of jet fuel, about 30% of which burned up outside the towers. The rest burned off in ten minutes, leaving nothing in the buildings but ordinary office fires.§

Before long, the fires were putting out black, smudgy smoke (as you can see at the top of the next page). This almost always indicates an oxygen-starved, low-temperature fire. Despite that, the South Tower collapsed just 56 minutes after being hit and the North Tower after just an hour and 42 minutes.

---

* http://tinyurl.com/WTCattack1

† http://tinyurl.com/WTCattack2

§ WTC lead investigator Shyam Sunder, quoted in Andy Field, "A Look Inside a Radical New Theory of the WTC Collapse," firehouse.com, 2/7/04, http://tinyurl.com/fieldfirehouse, cited (at a different web address) in David Ray Griffin, *Debunking 9/11 Debunking: An Answer to Popular Mechanics and other Defenders of the Official Conspiracy Theory,* Northampton MA: Olive Branch Press, 2007, p. 155; and NIST, *Final Report on the Collapse of the World Trade Center Towers,* p. 179, also cited in Griffin, p. 155.

If you're near a computer, go to the web-page in the footnote and look at a video or two of each of the towers collapsing.* (If you're not near a computer, go back later and check out the online videos and color pictures we direct you to; black-and-white pictures in a book just can't do the job. If you don't have access to a computer, this book will still make a complete, compelling argument, but you'll be missing some dramatic, convincing visuals.)

In every video, you'll see the parts of the towers below the impact zones collapse even-ly, steadily and rapidly—straight down through their centers, which should have been the path of greatest resistance—until there's virtually nothing left of them.

That brings us to our first problem:

* http://tinyurl.com/WTCvideos

Problem #1: Nothing *ever* falls into the path of greatest resistance.

If anything ever did, the word *resistance* would have no meaning. This is just common sense, since stopping things from falling through it (or blowing it over, or the like) is exactly what the resistance in a building is designed to *resist.*

If a fire destroys, say, half of a building, the building will—of course—topple *toward* the destroyed side; it won't collapse into the part of the building that's still standing, unburned and structurally intact. Like everything else, collapsing buildings fall *away* from the path of greatest resistance.

It's as if a treetop caught fire and instead of the flames slowly working their way down the tree, with branches breaking off and falling down through the air next to it, the entire burning top of the tree plunged *directly down through the intact trunk*...steadily and very quickly, right down to the ground.

What would you think if you saw that happen (other than, "Why didn't I have my video camera turned on?"). You'd immediately and automatically assume that the trunk of the tree must have somehow been suddenly—and completely—removed.

In the case of the Twin Towers, however, the path of greatest resistance wasn't something as insubstantial as a solid tree trunk—in each building it was 80,000 *tons* of structural steel.* Now look at those videos again, and watch the towers fall directly down through their centers (as well as scatter debris in a wide circle evenly around them). What happened to all that structural steel? Why didn't it stop the collapses, or at least knock them sideways off the center of the building (as started to happen with the South Tower)?

Problem #2: Fires don't suddenly destroy entire buildings, evenly and completely.

Natural fires are organic and irregular. They consume the fuel in one place and move on to another, allowing the first, burned-out zone to cool. The fiercest wind-whipped forest fires leave certain trees and houses completely untouched. Only artificially set fires can be made to burn even somewhat symmetrically.

Problem #3: Many steel-frame high-rises have experienced much larger, hotter and longer-lasting fires than those in the Twin Towers, but not a single one has ever collapsed.

On August 5, 1970, a severe fire and explosion devastated the top two floors of One New York Plaza in lower Manhattan. Although those floors burned for over six hours (more than six times longer than WTC 1 and more than three times longer than WTC 2), no part of the build-

---

* http://tinyurl.com/massandpe

ing collapsed. (For amazing color pictures of the fires we mention here, see the footnotes.*)

On May 4, 1988, a fire gutted four floors of the First Interstate Bank in Los Angeles. With large flames flaring out of the building's windows, it took 64 fire companies almost four hours to put it out (six times longer than WTC 1, more than twice as long as WTC 2). But the building did not collapse.

On February 23, 1991, eight floors of One Meridian Plaza in Philadelphia burned for *eighteen hours*—compared to 56 *minutes* for WTC 2 and 1h 42m for WTC 1. But there was no collapse.

On October 17, 2004, 26 floors of tallest building in Caracas, Venezuela (the East Tower of Parque Central) burned for *seventeen hours*—eighteen times longer than WTC 2 and ten times longer than WTC 1. Although high temperatures stopped firefighters from reaching the tower's upper floors, where the fire was strongest, the fire chief of Caracas later stated that there was no permanent damage to those floors. "Engineers have gone up there and inspected. It is very solid."

But why talk about *other* buildings? On February 13, 1975, the North Tower (World Trade Center One) *itself* experienced a fire more intense than it did on 9/11. The fire started on the 11th floor and eventually cov-

* http://tinyurl.com/firesinhighrises ;
http://tinyurl.com/skyscraperfires

ered seven floors (as opposed to six on 9/11) and burned for approximately three hours (almost twice as long as on 9/11). Harold Kull, captain of the New York Fire Department's Engine Company Six said, "It was like fighting a blowtorch." There were almost a hundred massive floors above the fire zone but the base of the North Tower supported them easily.

Ah yes, you say, *but those buildings weren't struck by planes.* So let's look at one that was:

On July 28, 1945, a B-25 bomber, fueled by high-octane gasoline, rammed into the 79th floor of the 102-story Empire State Building, the world's tallest building at the time. The fuel ran down stairwells and elevator shafts and ended up burning five floors; it took about three hours to put out.

There was substantial damage to the structure; in fact, one of the bomber's engines went straight through the building and fell out the other side. But although the Empire State (which was completed in 1931) used technology forty years less advanced than that in the Twin Towers, it didn't even begin to collapse.*

There have been many other substantial fires in modern skyscrapers and not a single one has ever caused a building to collapse.

Problem #4: The Twin Towers were built to withstand airliners crashing into them, widespread fires and just about anything else you can think of.

Whatever your opinion of the Twin Towers aesthetically, their structural engineering innovations were so extraordinary that the American Society of Civil Engineers gave them an award in 1971 for being the project that demonstrates "the greatest engineering skills and represents the greatest contribution to engineering progress and mankind."[†]

The Twin Towers' designers were well aware of the bomber that crashed into the Empire State Building. To safeguard against

---

* http://tinyurl.com/B-25empirestate

† Angus K. Gillespie, *Twin Towers: The Life of New York City's World Trade Center* (New Brunswick NJ: Rutgers University Press, 1999), p. 117

something like that happening again (as well as other threats), the towers were massively overbuilt, designed to withstand a fully loaded, fully fueled Boeing 707—the largest commercial airliner of the time—ramming into them at 600 mph.*

That's equivalent to the impact of the larger Boeing 767s that hit the Twin Towers on 9/11 at much lower speeds—even if they'd been fully loaded and fully fueled. But they weren't. Just 51% of the seats on the North Tower plane were occupied, and just 31% on the South Tower plane.[†] And since they were only flying from Boston to Los Angeles (nowhere near their maximum range), their fuel tanks weren't full either.

According to calculations made by the engineers who helped design the Twin Towers, "all the columns on one side of a tower could be cut, as well as the two corners and some of the columns on each adjacent side, and the building would still be strong enough to withstand a 100-mile-per-hour wind."[§]

As the late Frank DeMartini, former construction manager of the World Trade Center, puts it, "I believe that each [of the

---

* NIST, NCS NCSTAR1, p. 6, http://tinyurl.com/ncstar1 •
Also see *City in the Sky,* Times Books, Henry Holt & Co, 2003, p. 131

† http://tinyurl.com/hoffmananomalies

§ http://tinyurl.com/shouldhavestood

Twin Towers] probably could sustain multiple impacts by airliners because this structure is like the mosquito netting of your screen door...and the jet plane is just a pencil puncturing [it]. It really does nothing to the screen netting."

Both the towers were built around a core of 47 massive steel box columns, each 52" x 22"—about four feet by two feet—at the base. The sides of these columns were four inches thick at the bottom; braced with girders at least 30" deep, they carried about half the buildings' gravitational loads. With the safety factor built in, they were five times stronger than they needed to be. Around the edge of the buildings were an additional 240 perimeter columns, each a 14" steel box composed, at the bottom, of 4"-thick plates.*

Even if all the insulation had somehow been knocked off all the columns, the fires still wouldn't have been hot enough to do much damage. Aviation fuel is basically kerosene; if it could significantly soften steel girders, the top of your camp stove would melt every time you use it. Even in the very hot fire that started on the 11th floor of WTC 1 in 1975 (described on pp. 17–18), the columns didn't collapse, or even deform.

Under ideal conditions (in a controlled environment, with just the right mixture of oxygen), jet fuel can burn as hot as 1400°–1600° F.

---

* *Engineering News Record,* http://tinyurl.com/WTCgoingup

Office fires burn at about 600°–800° F. Steel doesn't melt until about 2750° F, and even when it's completely engulfed in flames, only a small portion of the fire's heat is transferred to it.

For a metal, steel is a relatively poor conductor of heat—you can hold a three-foot-long steel rod in one hand and cut the other end of it off with a torch without your hand getting hot. (Also, steel generally returns to its normal strength when it cools. In most cases, it's not permanently weakened by fire.)

Typical office fires burn out in about twenty minutes in any one location. So to soften a steel girder to the point where it loses half its strength, you'd need something far hotter—and far less mobile—than office or jet fuel fires.

Problem #5: How could the smaller, lighter top sections of the towers completely destroy the much heavier, stronger and completely undamaged sections below the impact zones?

Here's Jim Hoffman's concise summary of NIST's explanation of how the Twin Towers collapsed:

"The aircraft impacts dislodged insulation from the steel, and the exposed steel succumbed to the fires. Sagging trusses pulled in portions of the perimeter walls, causing a rapid spread of 'column instability' in the perimeter columns, which in turn strained the fire-weakened core columns. The 'tremendous energy' of the floors above the collapse zone led to 'global collapse.'" (NIST didn't say where that "tremendous energy" was supposed to have come from.)

In the case of the North Tower, NIST says the top twelve floors (99–110) began to behave—for some reason it doesn't explain—as a detached "rigid block" that fell abruptly onto the structure beneath it with such force that "global collapse began."* (As already mentioned, NIST doesn't carry the story beyond that point.)

Remember, the lower 92 stories were not damaged by plane impact or fire. What's more, since the building's columns got thinner as they rose, the lower 92 floors were much stronger than the upper twelve. (At the top of the next page is a comparison of a core column from floors 1 to 7—shown in dark gray, on the bottom—with one from floors 98 to 101—shown in light gray, on top.)

Yet, according to NIST, the weaker, lighter twelve-story block somehow generated enough energy to act as a "pile-driver"† to destroy everything below it. To do that, those twelve floors would definitely have had to remain a

---

* NIST's collapse hypothesis is outlined mainly in NIST NCSTAR 1-6, and in more detail in the subfile NIST NCSTAR 1-6D.

† NIST itself doesn't employ the term *pile-driver* but it's such an apt description of their theory that it's widely used by everyone else.

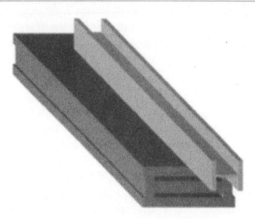

rigid block. If they broke up, they obviously wouldn't threaten the 92 intact floors beneath.

But *why* would they stay solidly together when encountering the stronger 92 floors below? Here's Kevin Ryan's take on it:

"NIST uses this concept of an upper floor 'rigid block' in its reports and presentations.* The idea implies that a pile-driver effect was possible. Questions I might ask about this rigid block include:

"1. How did the inward-bowing perimeter walls, which NIST said buckled to initiate collapse, sever so cleanly and symmetrically....?

"2. How was this rigidity measured and how was it different from the rigidity of the building below the impact zone?

---

* http://tinyurl.com/NIST2005;
http://tinyurl.com/NIST2005finalRpt

"3. How did the...top block meet the...lower block without [pushing] the top block off its vertical path?

"4. Once the upper section appears to be no more than dust (after only a few seconds), where is this rigid block and what is driving the [collapse]?"*

Even if those twelve stories somehow magically held together, they still couldn't have generated the energy required. There was nothing special about their weight—the lower part of the building had been holding them up without difficulty since 1970, and was designed to do so in a 140-mph hurricane.† So the energy needed to destroy the lower 92 stories would have had to come from the *velocity* of the upper block. It had to fall—hard—on the lower structure; a gradual buckling of columns and sagging of floors wouldn't do the job.

But even if the entire impact zone—floors 93 through 98—had been completely destroyed by the planes (it wasn't, of course, but we're trying to give NIST's theory its best shot) and the upper twelve stories dropped the entire six stories of the impact zone in free fall, the force they'd exert can't *begin* to account for the crushing of the 80,000 tons of structural steel below it, or the pulverization of 90,000 tons of concrete, or for the rapid expansion of

* email to Gregg Roberts, 4/20/11

† http://tinyurl.com/WTCdemolition

a massive dust cloud that covered lower Manhattan and billowed out over the Hudson River almost all the way to New Jersey.*

The story for the South Tower makes even less sense. Since the impact zone of the plane was lower—the 78th to 84th floors—the top section was larger, about 26 floors. But as you can clearly see in the photo on the front cover, it began its descent toppling off the lower part of the building. How could it crush the heavier, stronger 77 floors below it if it didn't even fall directly onto them?

Problem #6: How could the collapses be so perfectly symmetrical?

Each building had 110 floors; each floor was supported by 287 separate columns (47 in the core, 240 on the perimeter). That's a total of more than 60,000 column-to-floor connections. For the Twin Towers to have collapsed the way the videos show they did, each one of those 60,000+ connections would have had to disconnect at exactly the right instant; otherwise the buildings would have tipped one way or the other.

We won't waste our time calculating the odds against that happening by chance, but we imagine the resulting number would fill the rest of this book. (For that matter, what are the odds of 287 connections on a *single floor* all disconnecting at exactly the right instant?)

---

* http://tinyurl.com/massandpe

Look at those videos of the Twin Tower collapses one more time. Even though the impact of the planes and the damage caused by fires were random and uneven, the destruction of the buildings is *incredibly* symmetrical. The top of the North Tower seems to telescope effortlessly down into the intact portion of the building, and the collapse remains symmetrical from start to finish.

Although the top of the South Tower begins falling 22° off-center, to many people's eyes it appears to swing back into line. (It's hard to see through all the dust.) If it did realign itself, it's difficult to imagine what titanic force could have made it do that. And in either case, where did it end up? There was no 26-floor section of building—or the remnants of one—lying on the street next to the South Tower's debris pile. Did it just blow up in mid-air?*

Problem #7: Where are the floors?

If a 110-story building comes crashing down, pushing one floor in front of another—each about three feet thick and an acre in size—you'd expect to see, at the bottom, a huge pile of floors. Is that what you see at the top of the next page? (Use the firefighter in the front center for scale.)

Do you see a huge stack of floors? I see a bunch of rubble and some sections of outside

* http://tinyurl.com/symmetricalcollapse

wall sticking up at odd angles (they may have fallen from above and stuck in the debris). I don't see any floors, and neither did the Ground Zero workers; no intact floors, and very few significant parts of floors, were found at the bottom of either tower.

What could have brought these huge buildings crashing down if all 110 floors, each an acre in size, containing a total of 90,000 *tons* of concrete, disintegrated into dust before they hit the ground?

Problem #8: Where are the people?

In a gravitational collapse, you'd expect to find bodies crushed between the floors. There were about 2750 victims in the Twin Towers but only 300 whole bodies were found. Not only were the buildings turned to dust but so, apparently, were most of the victims.

More than eleven hundred of them remain completely unaccounted for; no pieces of their bodies have been collected large enough to get DNA samples from (and that doesn't take much). How could fire and a gravitational collapse account for such thorough devastation?

(In 2006, there was a gory footnote. More than 700 human bone fragments—each less than half an inch long—were found on top of the 40-story Deutsche Bank building, across the street from the South Tower. How did they get there, and how did they get to be so small?)

Problem #9: Where's everything else?

The Twin Towers contained about four million square feet of office space, in which there were tens of thousands of desks, chairs, computers, printers, cubicles, filing cabinets, telephones, light fixtures, water coolers, toilets, sinks— equipment of every conceivable sort. And what was in the wreckage at the bottom? Here's FDNY firefighter Joe Casaliggi:

"You have two 110-story office buildings. You don't find a desk. You don't find a chair. You don't find a telephone, a computer. The biggest piece of a telephone I found was half of the keypad and it was about this big [holding his thumb and index finger about 2½" apart]. The building collapsed to dust."*

Aside from steel columns and girders, virtually the entire buildings and their contents

---

* http://tinyurl.com/casaliggi

were turned to powder and tiny chunks of debris. A four-inch layer of dust covered all of lower Manhattan. Here's how NY Governor George Pataki described it: "The concrete was pulverized....All of Lower Manhattan, not just this site, from river to river, there was dust, powder....The concrete was just pulverized."*

And it was *finely* pulverized, much of it like talcum powder, in clouds that expanded to five times the volume of each tower in 30 seconds. (Sometimes such clouds of dust are referred to as *pyroclastic*, because they resemble the ones that pour out of erupting volcanoes.)

Ninety thousand *tons* of concrete and thousands of tons of office furniture, fixtures and equipment are missing from the debris pile at the base of each building. What sort of force could have destroyed all that?

Problem #10: Where did all the molten steel come from?

Problems 7, 8 and 9 mentioned various things you'd expect to find in the debris pile that simply weren't there. But there was also something there you *wouldn't* expect to find: tons of molten steel.

It started to appear even before the buildings collapsed. A flow of brightly glow-ing molten metal, accompanied by several smaller flows, appeared on the exterior wall

* http://tinyurl.com/Patakiwalk (It's mostly pretty boring; the
quote above begins at ~2:15.)

of the South Tower seven minutes before it collapsed.* And there's lots of other evidence of molten steel.

University of California professor Abolhassan Astaneh-Asl, the first structural engineer given access to the junkyard of WTC steel at Fresh Kills Landfill on Staten Island, said, "I saw melting of girders....If you remember the Salvador Dalí paintings with the clocks that are kind of melted—it's kind of like that. That could only happen if you get steel yellow-hot or white-hot."†

In the *Journal of the American Society of Safety Engineers,* Bechtel engineers, responsible for safety at Ground Zero, wrote that "the debris pile...was always tremendously hot. Thermal measurements taken by helicopter each day showed underground temperatures ranging from 400° F to more than 2800° F."§

The US Department of Labor stated that "even as the steel cooled, there was concern that the girders had become so hot that they could crumble when lifted by overhead cranes."** There's nothing in the official story to account for temperatures anywhere near that high—not burning jet fuel, office fires or anything else.

---

* http://tinyurl.com/SouthTowermolten

† http://tinyurl.com/astaneh

§ http://tinyurl.com/groundzeroanalysis ;
http://nasathermalimages.com

** http://tinyurl.com/groundzerodangerous

In a lecture at Stanford University on April 9, 2002, World Trade Center structural engineer Leslie Robertson stated: "There was a...little river of steel, flowing."* Many first responders and demolition workers saw the same thing:

"You'd get down below and you'd see molten steel—molten *steel*—running down the channel rails. Like you're in a foundry, like lava...like a volcano."

"We saw pools of literally molten steel."

"Steel flowed in molten streams."

"Molten steel was at the heart of the towers' remains."

"Molten metal red-hot weeks after the event."

"Beams had totally melted."

"Streams of molten metal that leaked from the hot cores and flowed down broken walls."

"Pieces of steel still cherry-red."

"Red-hot metal beams."

"Molten metal dripping from a beam."

"It looked like an oven...It was just roaring inside...a bright, bright, reddish-orange."†

The last fire in the debris piles wasn't extinguished until December 19, 2001—more than three months after 9/11.

---

* http://tinyurl.com/LeslieRobertson

† http://tinyurl.com/moltenmetal (and there's a transcript of sixty pages of their testimony at http://tinyurl.com/firefightertestimony)

Since NIST's version of what happened can't account for *any* molten steel, much less tons of it, they simply deny it existed. When asked about it, NIST's lead engineer, John Gross, said, "I know of absolutely nobody, no eyewitnesses who said so."* (See the previous page.)

Problem #11: What happened to FEMA Appendix C?

One of the few useful parts of the FEMA report, Appendix C,[†] documented conditions "capable of turning a solid-steel girder into Swiss cheese....Gaping holes, some larger than a silver dollar, let light shine through....A one-inch column [was] reduced to half-inch thickness," its edges "curled liked a paper scroll," having "been thinned to almost razor sharpness."[§]

Jet fuel and office fires can't burn hot enough to do that; nothing in the official scenario can. So NIST basically swept Appendix C under the rug and barely referred to it in their official report.

Problem #12: How did the buildings fall so fast?

If you dropped a bowling ball from the top of either of the Twin Towers just as they started to collapse, it would have hit the ground in

---

* http://tinyurl.com/grosslies

[†] http://tinyurl.com/FEMAreport

§ http://tinyurl.com/wpisteel

about 9.2 seconds. (That's *free fall.*) It's hard to get an exact figure with all the smoke and dust, but both towers appear to have collapsed in about ten to twelve seconds—fifteen at the most. (You can verify this yourself by looking at the videos with a stopwatch.)

Structures don't collapse at near free-fall acceleration unless virtually everything that resists their fall has been eliminated. If each floor had indeed collapsed onto the one below, there would have been a moment of resistance as each absorbed the impact of the ones falling on it from above. But there were no such jolts—the buildings collapsed smoothly.*

Problem #13: What were all those explosions?

New York City Fire Commissioner Thomas Von Essen ordered 502 firefighters and EMTs to record their experiences on 9/11 and afterwards; 12,000 pages of transcript were the result. When the *New York Times* requested the release of the transcript, the city resisted until the State Court of Appeals ordered them to comply.

One hundred and eighteen of the first responders reported hearing and/or seeing explosions. Here are a few of their comments:

It was "like on television [when] they blow up these buildings. It seemed like it was going all the way around like a belt, all these explosions."

* http://tinyurl.com/missingjolt

"With each popping sound it was initially an orange and then a red flash [that] came out of the building, and then it would just go all around the building on both sides."

"I saw a 'flash-flash-flash' and then it looked like the building came down."

"Pop, pop, pop, that's when I heard...the building coming down."

"Somewhere around the middle of the World Trade Center there was this orange and red flash coming out. Initially it was just one flash, then this flash kept popping all the way around the building and that building had started to explode."

"I thought the terrorists planted explosives somewhere in the building. That's how loud it was, [a] crackling explosive."[*]

None of these eyewitness accounts of explosions are noted in the final NIST report, even though NIST boasts that it interviewed a thousand witnesses.

Problem #14: What propelled huge steel beams great distances at high speed?

Girders weighing several tons were found 600 feet (two football fields) from the base of the North Tower. A gravitational collapse can't account for this. Things fall *down* in a gravitational collapse—they don't shoot out sideways, at least not very far or very fast.

---

* http://tinyurl.com/explosionreports

Using special software, physics instructor David Chandler analyzed video clips frame by frame, and placed markers so he could track particular projectiles. He was able to follow the paths of many objects and calculate their speeds; among them was a four-ton girder that was ejected horizontally at over 70 miles an hour. To do that takes as much energy as shooting a 200-pound cannon ball three miles.

But perhaps the most convincing evidence is what you can see with your own eyes. Go to the link in the footnote for a short video in which Chandler argues very convincingly, pointing things out in a repeating loop of the North Tower's collapse, that it was destroyed by explosions, not fire and gravity.*

As for the South Tower, the evidence is so clear you don't need a video to analyze it. Just look one more time at the photo on the front cover, with the top 26 stories toppling off the bottom of the building. Note the billowing clouds of smoke, the flying girders, the orange sprays of molten steel. If this is a gravitational collapse, they're going to have rewrite the laws of gravity.

---

* http://911speakout.org/?page_id=8 (it's the first video on his page). There's a lot of good stuff elsewhere on that website too—http://911speakout.org .

An explanation that actually fits the facts

You can see that the official version of what happened on 9/11 is as full of holes as a piece of Swiss cheese (or steel from FEMA Appendix C). There is, however, a more frightening explanation that eliminates every single one of the fourteen problems I've just described. It's that the buildings were destroyed by controlled demolition—the placing of thousands of explosives on columns and beams and then detonating them in a precise sequence.

Let's look at the evidence in the light of that explanation. In a controlled demolition, you hear the sounds of the explosives (called "cutter charges") going off, followed by a rapid symmetrical collapse through what *was* the path of greatest resistance—typically the center of the building, which has been sliced to pieces. Massive clouds of dust and smoke race away from the building at high speed.

(In a normal controlled demolition, you don't want beams flying into adjoining buildings, so you don't use enough explosives to do that, but it's easy enough to accomplish if for some reason you need that kind of power and don't care about the consequences to surrounding buildings.)

A typical controlled demolition uses high-energy explosives like RDX or C4, but they make a lot of noise and produce bright flashes of light. If you wanted to try to conceal what you were doing, you'd probably use *thermite* or one of its close cousins—military-grade incendiaries that cut through steel like hot knives through butter but are quieter and less visible than C4 or RDX (although they're still quite visible and loud).

Thermite can reach temperatures of over 4500° F in just two seconds (steel melts at 2750° F). Adding sulfur to thermite makes *thermate,* which produces even faster results.

Nanothermite (also known as *super-thermite)* is a mixture of ultrafine aluminum and iron oxide developed at highly advanced "national security" labs like Lawrence Livermore and Los Alamos. It explodes even more quickly. If you put nanothermite into a goop called *sol-gel,* it can be cast to shape, like clay. (As you might expect, nanothermite isn't commercially available, and it's not the sort of thing you can mix up in your backyard.)

All of these substances release enormous amounts of heat, which would account for the pools of molten steel and the red-hot beams and columns found in the debris piles, as well as the distorted pieces of steel full of gaping holes shown in the suppressed FEMA Appendix C.

And because they contain their own source of oxygen (or some other oxidizer), they burn just as well under water. That may be why the tons of water the firefighters were pouring on the WTC debris didn't do a lot of good, and why it took more than three months to put out the fires. ("You couldn't even begin to imagine how much water was pumped in there," said Tom Manley of the Uniformed Firefighters Association. "It was like you were creating a giant lake.")[*]

Dr. Steven Jones, a physicist formerly at Brigham Young University who was forced into early retirement for doing 9/11 research,[†] and an international team of scientists led by Niels Harrit of the University of Copenhagen, obtained four separate samples of dust from the WTC explosions. In all of them, they found small red/gray chips of unignited (and partially ignited) nanothermite.[§]

Dr. Jones and his team also found iron-rich microspheres in the dust. The largest ones were about a sixteenth of an inch in diameter but most were smaller across than a human hair. He calculates that there must have been about ten tons of them in all the WTC dust.[**] The only way such a huge quantity of them could form is if *lots* of molten steel or iron was aerosolized by an explosion.

---

[*] http://tinyurl.com/WTCfires

[†] http://tinyurl.com/unignitedthermite

[§] Niels H. Harrit, Jeffrey Farrer, Steven E. Jones, Kevin R. Ryan, Frank M. Legge, Daniel Farnsworth, Gregg Roberts, James R. Gourley and Bradley R. Larsen, "Active Thermitic Material Discovered in Dust from the 9/11 World Trade Center Catastrophe," *The Open Chemical Physics Journal,* pp. 7–31. (ISSN: 1874-4125. DOI: 10.2174/1874412500902010007), http://tinyurl.com/thermitepaper

[**] http://tinyurl.com/jonesarticle, p. 78

When Jones and his colleagues ignited some of the unignited nanothermite from the WTC dust, they were able to create very similar microspheres. The EPA also found microspheres in all their dust samples.[*] The engineering firm RJ Lee found that 5.87% of WTC dust was made up of these microspheres, as opposed to just .04% in dust collected from random buildings used as controls.[†]

At the 2007 Burning Man Festival in Nevada, John Parulis ignited 80 pounds of commercial thermite under a large steel sculpture of the word TRUTH. He then sent samples of the remains to Dr. Jones, who used electron microscopy to compare it to World Trade Center dust. The iron microspheres in both samples matched closely.[§]

Controlled demolitions destroy buildings (and their contents) suddenly, quickly, evenly and virtually completely—that's what they're *designed* to do. The buildings fall symmetrically down through their centers because the explosives are carefully timed by computers[**] to make them do just that—typically by cutting the core columns first.

---

* http://tinyurl.com/microspheres
    http://tinyurl.com/thermiticpyrotechnics
        http://tinyurl.com/explosiveresidues
            http://tinyurl.com/hightemperatures

† http://tinyurl.com/RJLeereport, table 3, p. 24

§ http://tinyurl.com/truthburningman

** Here's an example of one: http://hiex.bc.ca/products.html

There go all fourteen of the problems outlined in the previous chapter. Since controlled demolition accounts for *all* the evidence and the official story accounts for *none* of it, it's obviously worth investigating. But the government made it as hard as they could for anyone to do that.

The first rule at a crime scene is to preserve the evidence. As forensic fire-protection engineer Jonathan Barnett puts it: "Normally when you have a structural failure, you carefully go through the debris field, looking at each item, photographing every beam [where] it collapsed, and every column where it is on the ground, and you pick them up very carefully, and you look at each element."

But before FEMA's report came out in May of 2002, cleanup crews had shipped about 99% of the structural steel off to China as scrap metal, at the rate of about 400 truckloads per day.* Only a few hundred pieces avoided this fate.

But FEMA couldn't hide everything, and what remains is more than enough to completely discredit the official story. There isn't a jury in the country which, if presented with this evidence, wouldn't agree.

Only controlled demolition can account for the destruction of the World Trade Center buildings. If you *still* don't believe that, read the next chapter.

---

* http://tinyurl.com/WTCcleanup

Building 7—the ultimate proof

The destruction of the Twin Towers weren't typical controlled demolitions. For one thing, you normally want the whole building to fall into its own footprint, so it does minimal damage to surrounding buildings. But if you need to make it look as if buildings were destroyed by planes that struck them on high floors, you have to start the controlled demolition up there, instead of at the bottom as you typically would.

Since the detonators on cutter charges can be wireless and computer-controlled, there's no problem with doing this—you can create pretty much any scenario of destruction you want. But this is a much sloppier procedure and in the case of the Twin Towers, it created a 1200-foot-wide debris field around each building.

There was no need for such finagling with World Trade Center 7, the *third* high-rise destroyed on 9/11, at 5:20 in the afternoon, about seven hours after the Twin Towers. Since it wasn't struck by a plane, there was no need to begin the explosions at a particular point; a normal controlled demolition—one that started at the bottom, brought the building down directly into its own footprint, with minimal overlap into the streets, and compressed it into a four-story pile of debris—was perfectly adequate.

NIST's 2008 report on Building 7 says it was virtually engulfed by office fires. But videos show just eight to ten small, isolated office fires going on various floors at various times.*

According to NIST, the collapse began at column 79 on the 13th floor, due to "thermal expansion" caused by "a normal office fire"† below it, even though they state elsewhere in their report that "around 4:45 PM" [35 minutes before the building collapsed], the fire on "Floor 12 was burned out."§

What's more, the destruction of Building 7 looks *exactly* like a typical controlled demolition. Check out the link in the footnote for videos of some of those,** then compare the collapse of Building 7 side-by-side with another controlled demolition.††

Do you see any similarities? If you don't, you're definitely in the minority. Danny Jowenko, a top European controlled demolitions expert with 27 years experience, said of Building 7: "It's a controlled demolition....A team of experts did this....It's professional work, without a doubt."§§

---

* For a non-cherry-picked collection, search Google for "WTC 7 fires".

† NIST, NCSTAR 1A, p. 19

§ http://tinyurl.com/appendixL, p. L-26

** http://wtc7.net/videos.html

†† http://tinyurl.com/sidebysidedemolitions

§§ Just Google "Danny Jowenko 911".

And Hugo Bachmann, professor emeritus at the Swiss Federal Institute of Technology, says: "In my opinion, [Building 7] was, with the utmost probability, professionally demolished."*

At a "technical briefing" you needed permission to attend, David Chandler asked Shyam Sunder, NIST's lead WTC investigator, the following question: "Any number of competent measurements using a variety of methods indicate the northwest corner of WTC 7 fell with an acceleration within a few percent of the acceleration of gravity. Yet your report contradicts this, claiming 40 percent slower than free fall, based on a single data point. How can such a publicly visible, easily measurable quantity be set aside?"

Sunder basically avoided the question; you can judge his answer for yourself.† In its final report, however, NIST admitted that free fall occurred for a hundred feet or so of Building 7's collapse.§ But for free fall to have occurred, all 24 core columns and all 58 perimeter columns on several floors would have had to give way in a perfectly timed sequence; otherwise the building wouldn't have been in free fall at any point (and, coin-

---

* Ganser, Daniele, "Der erbitterte Streit um den 11. September," *Tages-Anzeiger,* 9/9/06 (http://tinyurl.com/ganserarticle), cited in Griffin, David Ray, "The American Empire and 9/11," *Journal of 9/11 Studies,* 4/07, http://tinyurl.com/griffinamemp .

† http://tinyurl.com/sundertalk, p. 16

§ http://tinyurl.com/NISTonfreefall

cidentally, would have toppled and not fallen smoothly and evenly straight down).

And then there's how *quickly* Building 7 came down—it collapsed in about 6.5 seconds. Huge clouds of dust can be seen racing away from it at 35 miles an hour. Steel that looks like Swiss cheese was recovered from it and lots of witnesses heard explosions. But for me the most compelling evidence that it was a controlled demolition—aside from the videos of it—is that *lots* of people knew it was going to happen before it did.

We hear FDNY Deputy Chief Nick Visconti, a 34-year veteran, announcing, before the collapse, "We're moving the command post over this way—that building's coming down." We hear a construction worker saying, "we're walking back because the building is about to blow up"; a police officer saying, "that building's about to blow up"; and another construction worker saying, "keep your eye on that building—it'll be coming down." And first responder and Air Force medic, Kevin McPadden, heard an actual countdown on a radio held by a Red Cross worker: *3...2...1...boom.**

Even more amazingly, Jane Standley of BBC TV managed to announce to a world audience that Building 7 had collapsed *twenty minutes before it happened.* You can see it

---

* http://tinyurl.com/kevinmcpadden
(Be sure to watch this one; it's amazing.)

standing in the window behind her as she makes the announcement.*

The BBC apologized for this "grievous error," citing the confusing events of the day. But how do confusing events make you psychic?

A mainstream news reporter, Jeffrey Scott Shapiro, wrote, "I was working as a journalist for Gannett News at Ground Zero that day, and I remember very clearly what I saw and heard....Shortly before [Building 7] collapsed, several NYPD officers and Con Edison [NYC's electric company] workers told me that Larry Silverstein...was on the phone with his insurance carrier to see if they would authorize the controlled demolition of the building—since its foundation was already unstable and expected to fall."†

Here's a comment on that from Alex Jones' Prison Planet website: "How did Silverstein expect to demolish the building safely when such a process takes weeks or even months to properly set up...? How could explosives have been correctly placed on such short notice inside a burning building?"§

---

* http://tinyurl.com/janestandley
† http://tinyurl.com/shapiroarticle , ¶5 and 8
§ http://tinyurl.com/jonescomment , ¶1

Building 7 housed offices of the CIA, the Secret Service, the Department of Defense, the New York City Office of Emergency Management, and the Securities and Exchange Commission (so the collapse destroyed thousands of files related to cases against companies like Enron and WorldCom). Other tenants included major financial firms.

It was, understandably, a highly secure building. How could al-Qaeda have gained sufficient access to set thousands of cutter charges? And where would they have gotten the extraordinary engineering expertise required to bring a 47-story steel skyscraper straight down into its own footprint?

That brings us to the end of the World Trade Center section of the book. If you'd like to see the Building 7 evidence tied together in full-motion and living color, there's a good ten-minute video at the link in the footnote.*

---

* http://tinyurl.com/aevideo (it's the second video down).

Other questions that need to be answered

Why did the US ignore warnings from at least nine other countries of impending al-Qaeda attacks?

The 9/11 Commission Report states that "the 9/11 attacks were a shock, but they shouldn't have come as a surprise. Islamic extremists had given plenty of warnings that they meant to kill Americans indiscriminately and in large numbers."[*] Later the report states that "during the spring and summer of 2001, US intelligence agencies received a stream of warnings that al-Qaeda planned, as one report put it, 'something very, very, very big.' Director of Central Intelligence George Tenet said 'the system was blinking red.'"[†]

Among the foreign governments and intelligence services that warned the US administration, CIA and FBI were Italy, France, Germany, Britain, Israel, Jordan, Egypt, Morocco, Afghanistan and Russia.[§] The warnings varied in their level of detail, but they all stated that they believed an al-Qaeda attack inside the United States was imminent. British

---

[*] *9/11 Commission Report Executive Summary*, p. 2 (Also see http://tinyurl.com/commission1 and http://tinyurl.com/commission2 .)

[†] *ibid*, p. 6

[§] Cameron, Carl, "Clues Alerted White House to Potential Attacks," Fox News, 3/17/02, http://tinyurl.com/cameronstory

Member of Parliament Michael Meacher listed the following warnings (all from 2001):*

- In March, Italian intelligence warned of an al-Qaeda plot in the United States involving a massive strike involving aircraft. (This was based on their wiretap of an al-Qaeda cell in Milan.)

- In July, Jordanian intelligence told US officials that al-Qaeda was planning an attack on American soil, and Egyptian intelligence warned the CIA that twenty al-Qaeda jihadists were in the United States, and that four of them were receiving flight training.

- In August, Israel's national intelligence agency, Mossad, gave the CIA a list of nineteen terrorists living in the US and said that they appeared to be planning to carry out an attack in the near future.

- That same month, the United Kingdom was warned three times of an imminent al-Qaeda attack in the United States, and the third warning specified multiple airplane hijackings. According to the Scottish newspaper the *Sunday Herald*, that report was passed on to President Bush a short time later.

- In September, Egyptian intelligence again warned American officials that al-Qaeda

* Meacher, Michael. "This war on terrorism is bogus," *The Guardian Unlimited – Comment*, 9/6/03 (London: Guardian Newspapers Limited). Retrieved 6/11/06. http://tinyurl.com/meacherarticle

was in the advanced stages of executing a significant operation against an American target, probably within the US.

In her testimony to the 9/11 Commission, Condoleezza Rice stated that "the threat reporting that we received in the spring and summer of 2001 was not specific as to time nor place nor manner of attack. Almost all the reports focused on al-Qaeda activities outside the United States."*

However, the President's Daily Briefing for August 6, 2001, titled *Bin Ladin Determined to Strike in US*, stated that "FBI information…indicates patterns of suspicious activity in this country, consistent with preparations for hijackings or other types of attack."† When asked about this at the 9/11 Commission hearings, Rice responded: "It wasn't something that we felt we needed to *do* anything about"!!§

One of the points sometimes made by defenders of the government's inaction is that the authorities would have needed precise details of the operation in order to take any protective measures against it, lest such measures shut down the country (the way it was shut down *after* the attacks, when it did no good). There would, of course, have been resistance to extreme measures without

---

* http://tinyurl.com/ricequote

† http://tinyurl.com/binladentranscript

§ http://tinyurl.com/911foreknowledge

strong evidence that an attack was imminent but, as we've just seen, the government *had* that evidence.

In any case, extreme measures probably wouldn't have been necessary. If security had simply been beefed up at airports and the most likely terrorist targets, and more fighters were put on alert in the Northeast Corridor (and the military exercises that moved them *out* of that area were canceled), that probably would have been enough. But the government couldn't even manage to send a couple of fighters to the World Trade Center after the first plane hit. (See pp. 56–57.)

Were those warnings in fact ignored, or was there actual foreknowledge of the attacks here in the US (and in other Western countries)?

Why did many Pentagon officials cancel travel plans on September 10?*

Why did San Francisco Mayor Willie Brown, who was booked to fly on September 11, receive a warning from his "security people at the airport" not to take the flight?†

Why did Scotland Yard prohibit Salman Rushdie from flying on September 11?§

---

* "Bush: We're at War," *Newsweek,* 9/24/01

† http://tinyurl.com/brownwarned

§ Doran, James, "Rushdie's air ban," *London Times,* 9/27/01, http://tinyurl.com/Rushdieairban

Why did two employees of Odigo, an Israeli-based instant messaging service, receive e-mail warnings of the attack two hours before it happened?*

Why were an avalanche of put options (highly leveraged bets that a stock's price will fall) purchased on the stocks of United and American, the two airlines whose planes were taken over on 9/11, in the days preceding the attack?†

And of course we've already discussed (on pp. 42–47) all the amazing evidence of foreknowledge in the case of Building 7: "That building's about to blow up"; "Keep your eye on that building—it'll be coming down"; the BBC's announcement that it had happened *twenty minutes before it actually did*; etc.).

How could hijackings so poorly planned be so incredibly successful?

Here's how one of the deans of 9/11 research, Jim Hoffman, describes it: "The attack scenario was irrational on the part of the alleged hijackers, and its execution is incomprehensible in light of their behavior....By flying from remote airports and going far out of

---

* http://tinyurl.com/odigoworkers

† http://tinyurl.com/911putoptions ;

http://tinyurl.com/putoptions2
(For the 911 Commission's argument that this surge in options was innocent, see http://tinyurl.com/911commissionreport .)

their way, the attack planners exposed their plan to almost certain ruin, had the air defense system operated normally.

"The originating airport for Flights 11 and 175 was Boston Logan instead of any of several airports near New York City. This created about 40 minutes of exposure to interception for each flight.

"Flight 77 flew to the Midwest before turning around to return to Washington DC. It was airborne an hour and 23 minutes before allegedly attacking the Pentagon. That would provide ample opportunity for interception even if the air defense system were mostly disabled.

"Flight 93 [also] flew to the Midwest before turning around to fly toward Washington DC. Had it reached the capital, it would have been airborne for more than an hour and a half. The odds of escaping interception with that plan would be infinitesimal under standard operating procedures.

"The behavior of the alleged hijackers preceding the attack is inconsistent with the skill and discipline needed to [pull] off such an attack. Apparently, Mohammed Atta barely caught Flight 11, [something] he was supposedly planning for years.

"The success with which hijackers allegedly took over four jets with knives and then piloted the jets to small targets is simply miraculous. None of the four flight crews were able to stop the alleged hijackers, in spite of several of the pilots being Vietnam veterans. None of the alleged hijackers were good pilots, yet the three buildings were hit with phenomenal precision."*

On the other hand, *Newsweek* reported that at least five of the supposed hijackers might have trained at US military bases.[†]

Were the supposed hijackers
even on the planes?

According to Hoffman, "no video of any of the nineteen hijackers at any of the three originating airports has been made public." In fact, there's little or no credible evidence that Arab hijackers were involved in the September 11th attacks at all, and substantial evidence that some of the ones named weren't involved.[§]

At a time when virtually every convenience store in the country had a security camera, Logan, a major international airport, apparently didn't have any in its departure lounges. Newark and Dulles did, but the FBI refuses to release video from any of them that might prove that the alleged hijackers actually boarded the flights.[**]

---

* http://tinyurl.com/hoffmananomalies ;
                    http://tinyurl.com/hanihanjour
† http://tinyurl.com/hijackerstrained

§ http://tinyurl.com/resurrectedhijackers
** "Logan Lacks Video Cameras," *Boston Herald,* 9/29/01

None of the flight crews on the four planes radioed Air Traffic Control about hijackings in progress, or punched in the four-digit hijacking code.* Flight Attendant Betty Ong made a call from American Flight 11. Only 4½ minutes of it have been made public, in which Ms. Ong described a stabbing but didn't mention Arab hijackers.†

Although they were supposedly devout Muslims, some of the alleged hijackers partied at topless bars and drank alcohol.§ And there's some evidence that at least six of them were still alive after the attacks.**

There's no public evidence that the remains of any of the hijackers were identified at any of the crash sites.†† And for the longest time, none of the contents of any of the four planes' black boxes were made public. (The government finally released data they said was from from Flight 77's flight data recorder, but there are questions about it.)§§

Why has the FBI shown so little concern for whether the hijackers have been correctly identified? The FBI director bragged, "We got the names right," as if merely pointing out who

---

* http://tinyurl.com/hijackingcode

† http://tinyurl.com/hoffmananomalies

§ http://tinyurl.com/carousingjihadists ;
http://tinyurl.com/carousers2

** http://tinyurl.com/hoffmananomalies

†† http://tinyurl.com/resurrectedhijackers

§§ http://tinyurl.com/novideos

on the flight manifests supposedly engineered the attacks was all they had to do—and despite the fact that he also said, at another time, that he thought the hijackers might have stolen other people's identities. (For links to news reports about this, and to a detailed discussion of it, see the footnote.*)

Where was the military response?

Despite normal intercept times of between ten and tweny minutes for errant domestic flights, the airliners commandeered on 9/11 roamed the skies for over an hour without interference.

According to one account, the FAA took eighteen minutes to even report Flight 11's loss of communication and deviation from its flight plan, and 39 minutes to report Flight 77's deviation from its flight plan. Despite the fact that Flights 11 and 175 were headed for

---

* "Hijack 'suspects' alive and well," *BBC News World Edition*, 9/23/01, http://tinyurl.com/hijackersalive • "Expert: Hijackers likely skilled with fake IDs," *CNN.com/U.S.*, 9/23/01, http://tinyurl.com/fakeIDs • Timothy W. Maier, "FBI Denies Mix-Up of 9/11 Terrorists," *Insight Magazine, Washington Times*, 6/11/03. The article was also published at www.insight-mag.com but the link is now dead. Prisonplanet.com mirrored it but that link is dead now too. A Google search produced a pull quote that didn't appear in Prison Planet's mirror: "The FBI now claims it always had the correct identities of the Sept. 11 hijackers, but others say that innocents became victims in the rush to name the perpetrators." (This still leaves this glaring issue of who actually committed the attacks completely unresolved.) • This footnote and its sources are adapted from Gregg Roberts, *Where Are the 9/11 Whistleblowers*, pp. 7–8, available from http://tinyurl.com/robertsessay .

New York City, interceptors weren't scrambled from nearby La Guardia but from distant bases instead, and only after long delays.

Two F-15s flying off the coast of Long Island weren't redeployed to Manhattan until after the South Tower was hit. Another two F-15s were scrambled from Otis AFB to protect Manhattan. The F-15s could have reached Washington from New York City in 9.6 minutes—long before the Pentagon was hit.

NORAD is the military defense shield that's supposed to protect the US from any form of airborne attack. Even though (according to one version of the story) NORAD received formal notification of the first hijacking at 8:38, and even though American Flight 77 was monitored on radar as it approached the capital, no interceptors were scrambled from Andrews Air Force Base in Maryland— *just eleven miles from the Pentagon*—until after it was hit at 9:38.[*]

Why wasn't the Pentagon better protected?

How could a commercial plane enter the Pentagon's "no-fly zone" without sending the correct transponder code? And if it didn't, why wasn't it intercepted before it reached what was probably the best-defended building in the world?

Why did the plane hit Wedge 1 of the Pentagon, which contained mainly newly ren-

---

[*] http://tinyurl.com/NORADstanddown

ovated and unoccupied offices? It was the only part of the Pentagon that had blast-hardened walls, and the offices of the top brass were on the other side of the building.*

Hitting the other side would have been simple but hitting Wedge 1 required a spiral dive so precise that veteran air traffic controllers thought they were watching a military jet, and experienced pilots still wonder if any human pilot could actually execute it.[†] The 500-mph final approach at tree-top level skimmed objects on the surrounding lawn and crashed the plane into the first floor of the building.[§]

How could an amateur pilot execute such an astoundingly complex maneuver? None of the alleged hijackers had ever flown jets. And Hani Hanjour, who was supposedly flying Flight 77, was particularly incompetent—so much so that one of his flight-school instructors refused to rent him a single-engine plane.**

It's impossible to imagine that there weren't video cameras constantly monitoring the Pentagon's walls and the surrounding land. Why hasn't the government released what those cameras recorded? The two segments they did release are almost comically

---

* http://tinyurl.com/Pentagonrenovation

† http://tinyurl.com/ATCsrecall

§ http://tinyurl.com/attackonPentagon ;
           http://tinyurl.com/hoffmananomalies

** "A Trainee Noted for Incompetence," *New York Times,*
           5/4/02, p. 10; http://tinyurl.com/hanihanjour

distant and indistinct. They show an explosion but no plane.*

Videos taken by businesses near the Pentagon were seized by the FBI shortly after the attack and weren't seen for the longest time. Finally, ones from the Sheraton hotel and the Citgo gas station were released. Not only are they of incredibly poor quality but it doesn't look like they would have shown the impact even if they were of high quality.

Finally, investigators weren't allowed access to the crash site until well into October.†

(Some people think that no plane actually hit the Pentagon and that the damage was caused by a missile or the like. I used to believe that but the evidence has convinced me otherwise. For a thorough discussion of this controversy, see the footnote.)§

Was Flight 93 shot down by our own fighters?

According to the official story, United Flight 93, the fourth jetliner, crashed near Shanksville, Pennsylvania at 10:03 am due to a struggle in the cockpit between the hijackers and passengers who rushed them. Although passengers did struggle to gain control of the plane, the actual cause of the crash

---

* http://tinyurl.com/DODvideos

† http://tinyurl.com/missingevidence

§ http://tinyurl.com/noplanetheory

seems to have been an air-to-air missile that hit it miles before it plowed into the ground. Here's the evidence for that:

In addition to the primary crash site, "a second debris field was around Indian Lake about 3 miles from the crash scene....More debris from the plane was found in New Baltimore, some 8 miles away from the crash....State police and the FBI initially said they didn't want to speculate whether the debris was from the crash, or if the plane could have broken up in midair."*

An engine core was separated from the main impact crater by about 2,000 feet. Some officials suggested that wind scattered the debris once it was on the ground, but a nine-mph wind couldn't have blown debris eight miles, or budged a one-ton engine an inch, much less more than a third of a mile.[†]

The map on the next page shows:

• the primary crash site (the impact crater)

• the location of an engine,
                    about 2,000 feet away

• the Indian Lake marina,
                    about three miles away

• New Baltimore, about eight miles away

---

* http://tinyurl.com/93blackbox ; http://tinyurl.com/93crashsite
[†] http://tinyurl.com/crashof93

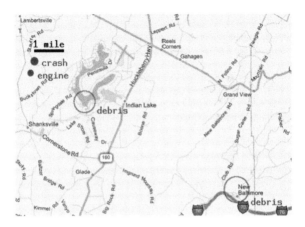

Aside from the widespread debris, which couldn't have been caused by a crash into the ground in a single location, eyewitness accounts jibe with the idea that the plane was destroyed in the air:

"I know of two people...that heard a missile. They both live very close, within a couple of hundred yards....This one fellow's served in Vietnam and he says he's heard them, and he heard one that day." The mayor added that F-16 fighter jets were "very, very close" to the airliner.

Laura Temyer, who lives several miles north of the crash site, was hanging clothes outside that morning when she heard an airplane pass overhead. "I heard like a boom and the engine sounded funny," she told a newspaper. "I heard two more booms, and then I didn't hear anything."

"I think the plane was shot down," Temyer says, who's twice told her story to the FBI. She adds that people she knows in state law enforcement agree that the plane was shot down and that decompression sucked objects from the aircraft, explaining why there was such a widely scattered debris field.

A passenger called 911 from the bathroom of Flight 93 to say that he heard "some sort of explosion and saw white smoke coming from the plane" but then 911 lost the connection.*

Why did President Bush stay sitting in an elementary school classroom reading a children's book after he'd been told the country was under attack † (and why did the Secret Service let him)?

Officials provided not two, not three, but *seven* different accounts of how Bush learned about the first plane hitting the World Trade Center.§ Do you have such a poor memory for how you learned about it?

For most people, it was like the Kennedy assassination: everybody who was over the age of five at the time of either event remembers *exactly* where they were and what they were doing when they heard the news. So if some-

---

* http://tinyurl.com/93witnesses

† *Fahrenheit 9/11* [film, 2004] (It's much more powerful to actually see Bush's reaction than to simply read about it.)

§ http://tinyurl.com/Bushon911

one says they don't, or has *seven different stories* about it, it begins to sound a little funny.

Here's how Jim Hoffman tells it (it's such an amazing story, I'll quote him at length):*

"George W. Bush had important business to attend to on September 11th: reading a book, *The Pet Goat*, with second-graders in Emma T. Booker Elementary School in Sarasota, Florida—ostensibly to promote his 'education program.' [He claims that b]efore entering the classroom around 9:02 AM, he was aware of the crash of Flight 11 into the North Tower. Later he said:

"'And I was sitting outside the classroom waiting to go in, and I saw an airplane hit the tower—the TV was obviously on, and I used to fly myself, and I said, *There's one terrible pilot.* And I said, *It must have been a horrible accident.* But I was whisked off...I didn't have much time to think about it.'†

"Since the only known footage of the North Tower impact was not played on TV until much later, [the only way his statement could be true is if] his Secret Service detail had...video from a secret camera trained on the North Tower at the time of the first impact [which would be even more suspicious].

"At 9:06, as Bush sat in front of the class, Andrew Card approached him, whispered

---

* http://tinyurl.com/Bushcoverstories

† http://tinyurl.com/CNNBushtranscript

something into his ear, taking less than two seconds. He is supposed to have told Bush that a second plane hit the towers. Bush looked momentarily befuddled. He did not ask his staff for further details. He remained seated and read out loud with the kids for at least eight more minutes, not leaving the classroom until 9:16.

"According to [journalist] Bill Sammon, 'The president noticed someone moving at the back of the room. It was White House Press Secretary Ari Fleischer, maneuvering to catch his attention without alerting the press. Mr. Fleischer was holding up a legal pad. Big block letters were scrawled on the cardboard backing: DON'T SAY ANYTHING YET.'*

"After leaving the classroom, Bush remained in the school to deliver a brief scheduled speech....[t]hen at around 9:33, his motorcade departed....In all, the comman-der-in-chief remained at Booker Elementary School for at least 29 minutes after he was informed that the nation was under attack. Why didn't he interrupt his photo op to respond to this emergency?....[W]hy did the Secret Service not immediately evacuate him to secure quarters, and why did he go on to give a speech at Booker, further publicizing his whereabouts?

---

* "Suddenly, a Time to Lead," *Washington Times,* 10/7/02,
http://tinyurl.com/bushreaction

"The time and location of the president's classroom photo op and speech had been publicized in advance. By 9:03, it was obvious that the nation was under attack, and that the mode of the attack was to use jetliners to strike high-value targets. The failure of the Secret Service to remove the president from his publicized location for a half hour implies either that [they] acted with extreme incompetence...(which resulted in no demotions or reprimands) or that [they had] insider knowledge that the attack would not include the president."

The danger to the president becomes even more obvious when you consider that the school where he spoke lies less than half a mile from the final approach path to Sarasota-Bradenton Airport (SRQ). A jetliner targeting the school and its occupants would have needed to divert from a normal flight path for just a few seconds to hit it, allowing no time for countermeasures.[*]

There are many more questions that need to be asked, but a book this size can only be an introduction. I've squeezed in as much as I could but I've still had to leave out lots of interesting and important material.

---

[*] http://tinyurl.com/Bushcoverstories

How is it possible?

Assuming you had a motive and the motivation to pull off an inside job of this size, how could you manage it? For example, how could explosives be placed in the Twin Towers without their 50,000 occupants knowing about it?

Well, first of all, you don't have to run wires—you can detonate charges remotely. (It's more expensive and there's usually no reason to spend the extra money, but it's a commercially available, well-tested technology.) So all you have to do is place the charges.

The Twin Towers' core columns are adjacent to the elevator shafts (or to utility rooms on the upper floors). If you were working on the elevators, you'd only have to (at most) saw through two layers of sheetrock to get to the core columns.

As it happens, in March 2001 the Ace Elevator Company began the largest elevator modernization in history at the Twin Towers.[*] This would have allowed access to the floor assemblies and columns for a significant period of time.[†]

Even without a large-scale maintenance operation, placing explosives throughout the towers wouldn't be nearly as hard to keep

---

[*] *Elevator World,* 3/01, http://tinyurl.com/elevatorproject

[†] http://911blogger.com/node/13272

secret as many people assume. White-collar workers going in and out of their offices pay little attention to what blue-collar workers are doing. Routine building maintenance requires access to the area above the ceiling tiles and even to the elevator shafts. In any case, the elevators were locked when they were being repaired and guards were stationed to prevent access to them.

What would have happened if someone had noticed something suspicious and reported it to building security? No one knows, but one company contracted to provide security for the World Trade Center in 2001 was Stratesec/Securacom. It first began doing work at the WTC in 1993, following the first World Trade Center bombing, and won a larger WTC contract in 1996.

For many years, George W. Bush's brother Marvin sat on Securacom's small board of directors, and it still included the president's cousin Wirt Walker III.* The company also provided security for Dulles Airport, where American Airlines Flight 77 took off that day, and for United Airlines. A fourth client was Los Alamos National Laboratory, where nanothermite, the explosive material discovered in the WTC dust, was developed.† (See pp. 38–40.)

---

* http://tinyurl.com/wirtwalker

† http://tinyurl.com/WTCaccess

The weekend before the 9/11 attack, the upper half of the South Tower was allegedly powered down with very little notice to tenants. Although that wouldn't have been enough time to plant all the explosive charges needed in that part of the building, it could have facilitated a last-minute rush job to get everything done.

So there's a brief overview of how destruction of the World Trade Center buildings would have been possible. In comparison, the other aspects of the attacks (the molasses-like military response, the shooting down of Flight 93, and so on) would have been much easier to arrange.

The government has a lot of power, and if power is all you care about, you can often bend a great deal of it to your will, with terrifying results. Obviously, we don't know all the details. That's exactly why we're calling for a new, thorough, independent investigation.

How could they keep it a secret?

More than 130,000 people were eventually employed in the Manhattan Project, yet it was kept quite secret for quite a while—despite the fact that the intelligence services of two very powerful enemy nations were doing their damnedest to find out about it. Between August 1942, when the Manhattan Project was formed, and August 1945, when it destroyed two Japanese cities, very few people, even in the nearby town of Santa Fe NM, knew what those 130,000 people were doing—in spite of the fact that they tested the first atomic bomb right inside the United States.

Even more relevant to 9/11 is Operation Gladio. (Technically "Gladio" just refers to activities in Italy but it's applied generally to ones all over Europe. The name comes from *gladius*, a type of Roman short sword—which is also where the word *gladiator* comes from.)

"After World War II, the UK and the US decided to create 'stay-behind' paramilitary organizations, with the official aim of countering a possible Soviet invasion through sabotage and guerrilla warfare behind enemy lines. Arms caches were hidden, escape routes prepared, and loyal members recruited: i.e., mainly hardline anticommunists, including many ex-Nazis or former fascists, whether in Italy or in other European countries....The anti-communist networks, which were present in all of Europe, including in neutral countries like Sweden and Switzerland, were partly funded by the CIA."*

"The origin of Gladio can be traced to the so-called 'secret anti-Communist NATO protocols,' which [allegedly committed] the secret services of NATO member states to work to prevent communist parties from coming to power in Western Europe...*by any means.* According to US journalist Arthur Rowse, a secret clause exists in the North Atlantic Treaty requiring candidate countries, before joining NATO, to establish clandestine citizen cadres...controlled by the county's respective security services...ready to eliminate communist cells during any national emergency."†

In Germany and Eastern Europe, the core of Gladio was the Gehlen Organization, named after Reinhard Gehlen, the Nazi general in charge of spying on Eastern Europe. After the war, the CIA made him an offer: *Hey, keep your network of spies and operatives in place and come work for us. We'll treat you even better than the Nazis did.* Gehlen eventually became West Germany's first head of intelligence.

---

* Fitchett, Joseph, "Paris Says it Joined NATO 'Resistance'", *International Herald Tribune,* 11/13/90

† Ganser, Daniele, "Terrorism in Western Europe: An Approach to NATO's Secret Stay-Behind Armies (162 KB PDF)," *Whitehead Journal of Diplomacy and International Relations,* South Orange NJ, Winter/Spring 2005, Vol. 6, No.1

Gladio agents set off bombs in train stations and other public places, killing hundreds of civilian men, women and children. The government blamed Communist and anarchist groups and was able to successfully influence public opinion thereby. Operation Gladio's cover was blown when one of the participants started getting too much attention from investigators in Italy and decided to publicly confess his role, but *for more than three decades*, this huge terrorist operation was a well-kept secret.*

The very fact that people think they *would* know about something as major as 9/11 being an inside job is one of the main things that helps keep that awareness out of their consciousness. Here's a nonpolitical example:

The Wright brothers' first successful flight, in December 1903, was long called a hoax by both the *New York Times* and the *Scientific American*. People believed that because they figured if the Wright brothers actually *had* flown, they surely would have read about it...in the *New York Times* or the *Scientific American*. Even as late as 1906, the Paris edition of the *Herald Tribune* could headline an article on the Wright brothers: "Flyers or Liars?"†

Mark Twain supposedly once said, "If you don't read the newspaper, you're uninformed.

---

* http://tinyurl.com/OpGladio • Philip Willan, *Puppetmasters: The Political Use of Terrorism in Italy* • Daniele Ganser, *ibid.*

† http://tinyurl.com/flyersliars

If you do read the newspaper, you're misinformed." The blow-dried airheads on TV don't help, as they chime in with, "Oh, that's just a *conspiracy theory*. Ignore it and watch this cute story about a cat that's learned how to knit."

And it isn't necessarily *just* ignorance either. Former Deputy CIA Director Frank Wisner used to refer to the media as "The Mighty Wurlitzer"—for his ability to make it play whatever tunes he wanted.*

(I'm not implying that the CIA was involved in 9/11. I'm just giving you an idea of how thoroughly some parts of the government control the mainstream media...or at least believe they do.)

---

* Mark Zepezauer, *The CIA's Greatest Hits,* Odonian Press, 1994, p. 52

Who would benefit?

I mentioned earlier that a real-estate investor named Larry Silverstein (in partnership with mall-owner Westfield America) bought a 99-year lease on the World Trade Center in late July 2001. Immediately afterwards, he took out a $3.55 billion policy with a consortium of insurance companies led by the giant Swiss Re; among other things, it covered acts of terrorism.

When the buildings were destroyed, Silverstein claimed that since two planes hit two different buildings, it constituted two separate acts of terrorism, and he was thus owed not "merely" $3.55 billion, but over $7 billion. He actually won that argument in court.* It's a little hard to figure out how much he eventually collected; there are lots of figures floating around—$4.6 billion, $5.6 billion, and so on. Whatever he got, it was certainly a lot more than he paid in premiums.†

However much Silverstein profited from 9/11, much bigger players and political considerations would obviously have been more important. After all, 9/11 has been used as an excuse to start two wars and to shred civil liberties, due process and the rule of law in the United States.

* http://tinyurl.com/silversteinpayout

† http://tinyurl.com/WTCowners

In 1997, a group of neoconservative hawks, many of whom later became key officials in the Bush Administration, formed an organization called the Project for the New American Century (or PNAC).* In September 2000, PNAC published *Rebuilding America's Defenses,* a policy paper that called for a massive military buildup, but cautioned that it would likely take a long time to accomplish that unless there were "some catastrophic and catalyzing event—like a new Pearl Harbor."[†]

Changing a nation's direction doesn't come cheap, but as Madeleine Albright once famously put it (referring to starving Iraqi children): "We think the price is worth it." Well, sure it is, if *other people* are paying it... and, somehow, they always are.

The "War on Terror" became an umbrella for previously undreamed-of levels of pork, unaccountability and corruption in government and industry. The Pentagon budget bloated to obscene levels and weapons manufacturers gorged on it. Vice President Cheney's company, Halliburton, got fat no-bid contracts to rebuild the infrastructure that American bombs were destroying in Afghanistan and Iraq. And the infamous (and enormous) "USA PATRIOT Act," obviously written beforehand and sitting in a

---

* http://911review.com/motive/pnac.html

† http://911review.com/motive/empire.html
http://tinyurl.com/pnacpaper, p. 51

drawer waiting for the right moment, passed Congress overwhelmingly.

The United States has been at war in Afghanistan longer than it's ever been at war anywhere, and Iraq will pass Vietnam to claim second place around the tenth anniversary of 9/11.* Trillions of dollars have been wasted, and many billions of those dollars are simply "missing."

Lots of people—lots of our fellow Americans—have profited enormously from 9/11.

---

* http://tinyurl.com/lengthofwars

Our government wouldn't do this to us.

If some parts of the government were involved in 9/11 (as it seems they must have been), it wouldn't have needed to be all that *many* parts. The government is huge and, as you may have noticed, one hand often doesn't know what the other is doing.

If 9/11 was an inside job, it was what's called a "false-flag operation." (The name comes from the old practice of flying a false flag on your ship in order to get close to the enemy, then hauling it down and raising your own flag as you began firing your cannons. Pretty scummy, huh?)

Today the term is used to refer to one group (usually a government) committing a crime but making it look like someone else did it. The 20th century was full of false-flag operations (and plans for them), although most Americans don't know much about them.

The real perpetrators of these attacks were able to preserve their anonymity for years, or decades, and there are doubtless false-flag operations we still don't know about. We've already discussed Operation Gladio on pp. 69–71; here are six other examples—the first three by the Germans and Japanese, the last three by the good old US of A:

The Mukden Incident

In 1931, Japanese officers blew up a section of railway to create a pretext for annexing Manchuria.

The Reichstag Fire

In 1933, Nazi agents set fire to Germany's own congressional building (the Reichstag) and blamed it on the Communists. This created a violent backlash that allowed the Nazis to consolidate their grip on political power (by passing laws similar to the Patriot Act, in the name of "national security").

The Gleiwitz Incident

In 1939, the Nazis fabricated evidence of a Polish attack against Germany to justify invading Poland.

Operation Ajax

In 1953, the US and Britain used false-flag and propaganda operations against the democratically elected leader of Iran, Mohammed Mosaddeq. Information regarding this CIA-sponsored coup has been largely declassified and is now available in the CIA archives.*

---

* Kinzer, Stephen, *All the Shah's Men: An American Coup and the Roots of Middle East Terror;* John Wiley and Sons (2003.
  • *Journal of the American Intelligence Professional* 48: 258.

Operation Northwoods

This 1962 plan called for false-flag actions that included sinking a boat filled with Cuban refugees, hijacking US passenger planes, using aircraft disguised as Cuban MiGs to shoot down US military planes, and sinking a US ship in the vicinity of Cuba. Cuba would be blamed for these actions, thus providing an excuse to invade it and overthrow Castro's Communist government.

The plan was put together by senior members of the Department of Defense, including the Chairman of the Joint Chiefs of Staff Lyman Lemnitzer, but President John F. Kennedy rejected it. (It came to light through the Freedom of Information Act and was publicized by James Bamford.)*

The Gulf of Tonkin incident

In 1964, President Lyndon Johnson falsely claimed that North Vietnamese vessels had attacked US ships without provocation. This led to the Gulf of Tonkin Resolution, which committed the US to more than eight years of war in Vietnam, with millions of Vietnamese and 58,000 American soldiers dead. The results of 9/11 don't come close...yet.

---

* http://tinyurl.com/Northwds

People calling for a new investigation

If you're convinced that the official story simply doesn't hold water, you're not alone—not by a long shot. Here are a few of the people who are calling for a new, independent investigation.*

Senator Max Cleland, US senator from Georgia, 1997–2002. Former Army captain; awarded the Silver Star and Bronze Star for bravery; triple amputee from war injuries.

In the *New York Times* (10/26/03), he said: "As each day goes by, we learn that this government knew a whole lot more about these terrorists before September 11 than it has ever admitted."

In the *Boston Globe* (11/13/03), he said: "If this decision [to limit access to White House documents] stands, I—as a member of the [9/11] Commission—cannot look any American in the eye, especially family members of victims....This investigation is now compromised....This is *The Gong Show*; this isn't protection of national security."

Cleland resigned from the 9/11 Commission in December 2003, after having

* http://www.patriotsquestion911.com (We can't vouch for the accuracy of every one of the thousands of listings on this site, but since it gives citations for all of its quotes, you can check things out for yourself.)

served twelve months. On *Democracy Now* (3/23/04), he said: "One of these days we will have to get the full story because the 9/11 issue is so important to America. But the [Bush] White House wants to cover it up."

Raymond L. McGovern, 27-year CIA veteran. Former chairman, National Intelligence Estimates (NIE), the consensus reports of all US intelligence agencies. (According to the Office of the Director of National Intelligence, NIE's "are the intelligence community's most authoritative written judgments on national security issues.") He was responsible for preparing and presenting the President's Daily Brief (PDB) to Presidents Ronald Reagan and George H. W. Bush and for providing intelligence briefing to their vice-presidents, secretaries of state, the joint chiefs of staff and many other senior government officials. Upon retirement in 1990, McGovern was awarded the CIA's Intelligence Commendation Medallion and received a letter of appreciation from President George H.W. Bush.

In a blurb endorsing the book *9/11 and American Empire (Vol. I)—Intellectuals Speak Out*, McGovern wrote: "It has long been clear that the Bush-Cheney administration cynically exploited the attacks of 9/11 to promote its imperial designs. But the present volume confronts us with compelling evidence for an even more disturbing conclusion: that the 9/11 attacks were themselves orchestrated by this administration precisely so they could be thus exploited. If this is true, it is not merely the case...that the stated reason for attacking Iraq was a lie. It is also the case that the whole 'War on Terror' was based on a prior deception."

McGovern signed a petition requesting a reinvestigation of 9/11 and in a video interview on 7/22/06 stated: "I think...there's a cover-up. The 9/11 report is a joke. The question is: 'What's being covered up?'...[T]here are a whole bunch of unanswered questions. And the reason they're unanswered is because [the Bush A]dministration will not answer the questions....I think...that's certainly an impeachable offense."

Michael Scheuer, chief of the CIA's bin Laden unit at the Counterterrorism Center, 1996–99. After a 22-year CIA career, he's currently an author, political analyst, media commentator and adjunct professor of Security Studies at Georgetown University. His books include *Through Our Enemies' Eyes: Osama bin Laden, Radical Islam, and the Future of America* (2002, originally published anonymously); *Imperial Hubris: Why the West is Losing the War on Terror* (2004, originally published anonymously); and *Marching Toward Hell: America and Islam After Iraq* (2008).

On *Fox News* (on 10/9/10), Judge Andrew Napolitano asked Scheuer, "Was the 9/11 Commission report a whitewash?"

Scheuer replied, "It was a whitewash and a lie from top to bottom."

Major Scott Ritter, Marine Corps intelligence officer and chief weapons inspector for the United Nations Special Commission in Iraq, 1991–98.

In a video recorded 1/19/08, he stated that "we have an absolute requirement to know what happened on 9/11....No stone should be left unturned....[T]here must be a re-opening of the investigation, so that we the people of the United States know what occurred on that horrific day. And that way it lays to rest all conspiracies. We'll find out what happened.

"Did Bush and Cheney plan the demise of the building? Was this a terrorist attack by al-Qaeda? Or was it something in between? We frankly don't know....Let's admit that we didn't get a good report. Let's go out there and get the best report possible. And let's get to the truth so we know exactly what happened."

Robert Baer, a 21-year CIA veteran (and winner of the Career Intelligence Medal) on whose memoir the film *Syriana* was based. Pulitzer-Prize-winning journalist Seymour Hersh wrote that he "was considered perhaps the best on-the-ground field officer in the Middle East." Baer has written two nonfiction books about

CIA operations, *See No Evil* and *Sleeping with the Devil*, and the novel *Blow the House Down*.

In the British paper *The Guardian* (1/12/02), he's quoted as saying: **"Did bin Laden act alone, through his own al-Qaeda network, in launching the attacks? About that I'm...certain and emphatic: No."**

In an interview on *The Thom Hartmann Show* (6/9/06), Hartmann asked: "Are you of the opinion there was an aspect of 'inside job' to 9/11 within the US government?"

Baer: There is that possibility. The evidence points at it.

Hartmann: And why is it not being investigated?

Baer: Why isn't the WMD story being investigated? Why hasn't anybody been held accountable for 9/11?....Why have there been no political repercussions? Why hasn't there been...any sort of exposure on this? It really makes you wonder.

And in an article on rawstory.com (2/28/08), he stated: "There are enough discrepancies and unanswered questions in the 9/11 Commission Report that under a friendly administration, the 9/11 investigation should be re-opened."

Louis Freeh, director of the FBI, 1993–2001. Former US district court judge, assistant US attorney, FBI agent and officer in the Army JAG Corps Reserve.

In an essay in *Wall Street Journal* titled "An Incomplete Investigation" (11/17/05), he wrote: "Even the most junior investigator would immediately know that the name and photo ID of Atta in 2000 is precisely the kind of tactical intelligence the FBI has many times employed to prevent attacks and arrest terrorists. Yet the 9/11 Commission inexplicably concluded that it 'was not historically significant.' This astounding conclusion... raises serious challenges to the commission's credibility and, if the facts prove out, might just render the commission historically insignificant....No wonder the 9/11 families were outraged by these revelations and called for a new commission to investigate."

On CNN's *Lou Dobbs Tonight* (11/30/05), Dobbs asked: "Was the FBI ever given any reason to sense that there...would be an attack or some relationship to Mohammed Atta?"

Freeh answered: "Absolutely not....[w]e had [Department of Defense] officers...who made appointments... to go to the FBI and share this intelligence in 2000 and those appointments were canceled. It had to be...very powerful...information to make these officers...breach the chain of command

and go directly to the FBI. We'd like to know why those appointments were canceled."*

The people quoted above are just six of the thousands listed at patriotsquestion911.com . As of this writing (May, 2011), they also include:

• 220+ senior military, law enforcement, intelligence and government officials, including former vice-president Walter Mondale; senators Patrick Leahy, Chuck Schumer and Kirsten Gillibrand; former senators Bob Kerry, Mike Gravel, Lincoln Chafee, Bob Graham and Mark Dayton; congressmen Dennis Kucinich and Ron Paul; former US attorney general Ramsey Clark; and former commerce secretary Norm Mineta

• 300+ 9/11 survivors and family members

• 250+ military and commercial pilots and other aviation professionals

• 400+ medical professionals

• 400+ academics, including Lynn Margulis, Daniel Berrigan, Michael Parenti, the late

---

* The editor of www.patriotsquestion911.com added this note (which I've edited): *The 9/11 Commission Report asserts that only three of the alleged hijackers were known to U.S. intelligence agencies prior to 9/11: Nawaf al-Hazmi, Salem al-Hazmi and Khalid al-Mihdar. It doesn't mention that the names and photographs of alleged hijackers Marwan al-Shehhi and Mohamed Atta had been identified by a Department of Defense antiterrorist program more than a year prior to 9/11, and that they were known to be affiliates of al-Qaeda.*

Howard Zinn, Marcus Raskin, David Ray Griffin, Peter Dale Scott, Ralph Metzner and Lester Grinspoon

• hundreds of broadcasters, reporters, authors and publishers like Gore Vidal, Ralph Nader, Jim Hightower, Daniel Ellsberg, the late Peter Jennings, Graydon Carter, Lewis Lapham, Naomi Wolff, Erica Jong, Frances Moore Lappé, Dario Fo, Bob Scherr, Whitley Streiber, Janeane Garofalo, Randi Rhodes, Rosie O'Donnell, Thom Hartmann and Michael Moore, and

• actors, directors and musicians like Willie Nelson, Martin Sheen, Sharon Stone, Woody Harrelson, Mark Ruffalo, James Cromwell, James Brolin, Ed Asner, Peter Coyote, Harry Belafonte, Juliette Binoche, Marion Cotillard, David Lynch, Roseanne Barr, Charlie Sheen, Dick Gregory, Richie Havens, Ed Begley Jr, Daniel Sunjata, Michelle Phillips and Mos Def.

But perhaps the most impressive lists are at ae911truth.org . More than 1500 architects and engineers (with more than 25,000 years of professional experience), and more than 12,000 other supporters, are listed there, and they've all signed a petition demanding that Congress hold a truly independent investigation.

(I'm one of the 12,000+, and given how carefully they checked to make sure I was who I said I was, I can only imagine what they put the architects and engineers through. I know they verify every degree and credential.)

As we said at the start, you don't need an advanced degree to follow any of this—just a little common sense. But you may have been saying to yourself, *Yes, this all sounds convincing, but I'm not an architect or an engineer. How do I know I'm not missing something, or being misled?* So let's end this chapter by hearing from some people who *do* have advanced degrees and credentials in the relevant fields:

The American Institute of Architects is a distinguished organization and its most prestigious honor is the designation of "Fellow," which is awarded to members who've made contributions of national significance to the profession. Only about 2% of AIA members are Fellows and Daniel B. Barnum is one of them. Here's what he has to say about the Twin Towers:

"I have known from Day One that the buildings were imploded and that they could not and would not have collapsed from the damage caused by the airplanes that ran into them."*

Here's what another AIA member, Andrew Wolff, has to say: "The free-fall collapse of the fire-protected steel-frame structure of World Trade Center 7 could not have

* http://www2.ae911truth.org/profile.php?uid=999974

been caused by the limited structural damage and office fires which were observed prior to collapse. The actual scientific/forensic evidence (i.e. thermate particles in the dust and molten steel during debris extraction) calls into question the [NIST] report and points to a professionally controlled demolition by incendiary devices."*

And here's Alan C. Gray, "a mechanical engineer with 28 years of engineering experience....I've had extensive training in root cause investigations....The top of [WTC] Tower 2 should have fallen over rather than...down through the strongest part of the building"† (as you can clearly see from the photo on the front cover).

* http://www2.ae911truth.org/profile.php?uid=999974

† http://www2.ae911truth.org/profile.php?uid=985658

Conclusion

I could go on citing experts forever, but if all the evidence presented in this book still hasn't convinced you that there's a lot we don't know about 9/11, what will? And if nothing will, what do you have to fall back on? You've already seen that the official story makes no sense.

Yes, it's scary to conclude that 9/11 was an inside job. In fact, it's terrifying. But it's not, unfortunately, unbelievable. Think of Operation Gladio (pp. 69–71) or the Tonkin Gulf Resolution (p. 78).

By now more people have probably died prematurely from breathing the air around Ground Zero than died in the World Trade Center buildings themselves, and that's because Christine Todd Whitman, head of the EPA at the time, told them it was perfectly safe.* If a hack politician can kill thousands of people simply by parroting a facile lie, what can a dedicated group of political operatives achieve?

Plenty. And pretending they can't—or won't—isn't going to stop them.

There's nothing we can do now to help all the people who've died as a result of 9/11. But there *are* ways to stop similar things

---

* http://tinyurl.com/whitmanlied

from happening in the future, and one of them is to demand a new, thorough, independent investigation of 9/11. Don't vote for anyone who doesn't support it, and tell your friends what you've learned from this book (even if they roll their eyes and try to contemptuously dismiss it).

As Supreme Court Justice Louis Brandeis famously put it, "Sunlight is the best disinfectant." We need a whole lot more of it.

Other sources of good information

Here are some websites that generally provide good, reliable information:

• Architects & Engineers for 9/11 Truth,
http://ae911truth.org

• 9-11 Research, *http://911research.wtc7.net*

• 9-11 Review, *http://911review.com*
Especially interesting are
http://911review.com/denial/bigtent.html
and *http://911review.com/errors/index.html* ,
but watch out for the unreliable site *911review.org* .

• Scholars for 9/11 Truth and Justice
http://stj911.org

• Journal of 9/11 Studies
www.journalof911studies.com

• *911blogger.com*

• The Complete 9/11 Timeline
http://tinyurl.com/completetimeline

• Firefighters for 9-11 Truth
http://firefightersfor911truth.org

• The World Trade Center Environmental
Organization, *http://wtceo.org*

• *http://www.pleuralmesothelioma.com*

For DVDs, check out the annotated list at
http://tinyurl.com/good911dvds .

Since there's so much information online (you
could easily spend a month exploring the websites
listed above), and since video images are so visual-
ly compelling and convincing, you probably won't
need another book. But if you're curious about
what's available, check out the annotated list at
http://tinyurl.com/good911books .

Glossary

beam
A horizontal support member in a building

Building 7
World Trade Center Seven *(WTC 7)*, a 47-story sky-scraper destroyed on September 11, 2001 in a classic controlled demolition most people aren't even aware of

column
A vertical support member in a building

controlled demolition
Intentionally destroying a building by careful placement of precisely timed explosive charges

core column
A *column* in the center of a building

EMT
An emergency medical technician

FEMA
The Federal Emergency Management Agency

FDNY
New York City's Fire Department

first responder
A firefighter, *EMT,* police officer or anyone else whose job involves responding immediately to emergencies

Flight 11
The American Airlines flight that crashed into *WTC 1* at 8:47 am on September 11, 2001

Flight 77
The American Airlines flight that apparently crashed into the Pentagon at 9:38 am on September 11, 2001

Flight 93
The United Airlines flight that was apparently shot down over western Pennsylvania at about 10 am on September 11, 2001

Flight 175
The United Airlines flight that crashed into *WTC 2* at 9:03 am on September 11, 2001

floor truss
A *truss* that supports a floor *(that was easy)*

free-fall acceleration
How fast gravity pulls an object through a vacuum in the absence of obstructions (or other forces acting on it)

girder
A large steel *beam*

NIST
The National Institute of Standards and Technology

the North Tower
World Trade Center One *(WTC 1),* a 110-story office building in lower Manhattan that was destroyed on September 11, 2001

path of greatest resistance
Just what it says—the path (in the case of collapsing structures, the vertical path) that most strongly resists something moving through it

perimeter column
A *column* on the outside of a building

Port Authority
The Port Authority of New York and New Jersey, the public agency that owns *the World Trade Center* and leased it to a consortium headed by Larry Silverstein in the summer of 2001

the South Tower
World Trade Center Two *(WTC 2)*, a 110-story office building in lower Manhattan that was destroyed on September 11, 2001

truss
A rigid, open framework that supports a roof or a floor

the Twin Towers
World Trade Center One *(WTC 1)* and World Trade Center Two *(WTC 2)*, the North and South Towers

the World Trade Center
A complex of office buildings in lower Manhattan, most of which were completed around 1970

WTC 1
The *North Tower,* World Trade Center One a 110-story office building in lower Manhattan that was destroyed on September 11, 2001

WTC 2
The *South Tower,* World Trade Center Two a 110-story office building in lower Manhattan that was destroyed on September 11, 2001

WTC 7
World Trade Center Seven (also called simply *Building 7),* a 47-story skyscraper that was destroyed on September 11, 2001 in a classic controlled demolition most people aren't even aware of

Acknowledgments

This book could not have been written without the tireless assistance and wide-ranging technical knowledge of Gregg Roberts, who was virtually a co-author. If you're looking for a great researcher, he can be reached at gregg@wtc7.net.

Richard Gage, AIA, founder of Architects & Engineers for 9/11 Truth, and other members of its team provided valuable technical support and information regarding the World Trade Center. I also appreciate feedback and help received from other 9/11 researchers: Jim Hoffman, Kevin Ryan and Steven Jones.

Ty Koontz put together an index that should win some sort of prize. Unlike the sorry excuses for indexes in most books, this one is *complete.* If you look something up in *this* index, you'll *find* it.

Charlie Winton, my publisher, was a wise and steady hand on the tiller in what were sometimes tumultuous seas. Julie Pinkerton was a joy to work with. She responded to my emails so quickly it sometimes almost felt as if we were sitting in the same room talking.

My agent, Peter Beren, made it possible for this series of books to rise from the dead (or at least the critcally ill). I'm grateful to him for that, and I hope you are too.

The glamorous and sagacious Meridyth Duerr, and the somewhat-less-glamorous but equally sagacious Charlie Roach, kept my body (more or less) in shape through the many hours of sitting that writing a book demands.

The ultra-competent and super-responsible Paul Young did the same for my house (which was in even worse shape). Without Karen Bodding's dependability and attention to detail, I'd be completely lost.

My friends Meg, Linda and Ty guided me through a trying romantic relationship of a sort that, despite my antiquity, I'd never encountered before (I thought I'd seen them all). Without their wisdom and support, I never would have been able to focus on this book. Thanks, guys.

For help too varied to specify but greatly appreciated in every case, I'd like to thank Mark, Todd & Sarah, Zack, Jeff, Katie, Andy, Pierrette & Jean, Valerie, Carolina, Tom, Boyd, Marty and Jack.

About the author

Arthur Naiman has authored, co-authored, edited and/or published more than thirty books. In each of those categories, his books have sold millions of copies.

His first bestseller was *Every Goy's Guide to Common Jewish Expressions* (which he keeps meaning to put back into print). But he's probably most famous for *The Macintosh Bible,* which he created, edited and published the first four editions of (and wrote most of as well).

The Macintosh Bible was chosen Best Computer Book of 1994 by the Boston Computer Society, at a time when fewer than 5% of personal computer users had Macs (and thus had any use for the book). It must also be the only computer book that's ever been described, in an unsolicited reader's comment, as being "better than sex."

Naiman founded two publishing companies and started the Real Story Series—short, readable books on political subjects. Although only fourteen previous titles have been published in the series, 875,000 copies of Real Story books are in print worldwide.

TinyURL conversions

Many of the web addresses in this book (or, to use the technical term for them, URLs—*universal resource locators*) were too long to fit on a single line, or were just too tedious or tricky to type. In such cases, I took advantage of the wonderful service provided at http://tinyurl.com, which lets you assign shorter URLs to longer ones and then redirects anyone who uses the shorter URL to the correct webpage.

Although tinyurl.com seems very solid, anything on the web is subject to hacking. So here, as a precaution, are all the tinyURLs I used, listed by page number, and the actual, longer addresses they're supposed to forward you to. (Of course those longer addresses might change too, but there's nothing I can do about that.)

p. 4 • http://tinyurl.com/farmersquote ⤮ http://more.stltoday.com/stltoday/
entertainment/reviews.nsf/book/story/ab0778ad6967637f
86257627007f18e5?OpenDocument

p. 7 • http://tinyurl.com/FEMAinvestigation ⤮ http://www.fireengineering.com/
index/welcomeRB.articles.fire-engineering.volume-155.issue-1.departments.
editors-opinion.elling-out-the-investigation.html?cName=rbfirecone

p. 8 • http://tinyurl.com/kevinryan1 ⤮
http://www.globalresearch.ca/index.php?context=va&aid=5071

p. 9 • http://tinyurl.com/commission1 ⤮
http://911research.wtc7.net/post911/commission/index.html

• http://tinyurl.com/commission2 ⤮
http://911research.wtc7.net/post911/commission/report.html

p. 10 • http://tinyurl.com/NISTexec ⤮
http://wtc.nist.gov/pubs/NCSTAR1ExecutiveSummary.pdf

• http://tinyurl.com/NISTresponse ⤮ http://www.journalof911studies.com/
volume/2007/NISTresponseToRequestForCorrectionGourleyEtal2.pdf?

• http://tinyurl.com/grazkeeling ⤮
http://www.kfunigraz.ac.at/imawww/keeling/wtc/wtc.html

• http://tinyurl.com/collapsemodel ⤮ http://911research.wtc7.net/wtc/models

• http://tinyurl.com/NISTsFAQ ⤮
http://wtc.nist.gov/pubs/factsheets/faqs_8_2006.htm

• http://tinyurl.com/FAQreply ⤮
http://911research.wtc7.net/reviews/nist/WTC_FAQ_reply.html

p. 11 • http://tinyurl.com/NISTcant ⤮ http://journalof911studies.com/
volume/2007/NISTresponseToRequestForCorrectionGourleyEtal2.pdf

• http://tinyurl.com/kevinryan2 ⤮
http://www.journalof911studies.com/articles/Article_1_Ryan5.pdf

p. 12 • http://tinyurl.com/ryanfired ⤮
http://www.911truth.org/article.php?story=20041112144051451

• http://tinyurl.com/ultestingryan ⤮ http://ultruth.wordpress.com/2011/03/19/
u-l-s-testing-procedures-helped-make-that-possible/

9/11 → THE SIMPLE FACTS   ARTHUR NAIMAN

p. 12 • http://tinyurl.com/ryanfired2 ↦
> http://www.historycommons.org/entity.jsp?entity=kevin_ryan
• http://tinyurl.com/bettermirage ↦
> http://911research.wtc7.net/essays/nist/index.html
• http://tinyurl.com/collapsetheories ↦
> http://911research.wtc7.net/talks/collapse/index.html

p. 13 • http://tinyurl.com/WTCattack1 ↦
> http://911research.wtc7.net/wtc/attack/wtc1.html
• http://tinyurl.com/WTCattack2 ↦ http://911research.wtc7.net/wtc/attack/wtc2.html
• http://tinyurl.com/fieldfirehouse ↦ http://www.firehouse.com/news/news/look
> -inside-radical-new-theory-wtc-collapse

p. 14 • http://tinyurl.com/WTCvideos ↦
> http://911research.wtc7.net/wtc/evidence/videos/index.html

p. 16 • http://tinyurl.com/massandpe ↦
> http://911research.wtc7.net/papers/urich/MassAndPeWtc1.htm

p. 17 • http://tinyurl.com/fireinhighrises ↦
> http://911research.wtc7.net/wtc/analysis/compare/fires.html
• http://tinyurl.com/skyscraperfires ↦ http://ae911truth.org/news/41-articles/363-
> burning-question-should-the-history-of-high-rise-fires-be-ignored.html

p. 19 • http://tinyurl/com/B-25empirestate ↦ http://www.damninteresting.com/
> the-b-25-that-crashed-into-the-empire-state-building

p. 20 • http://tinyurl.com/ncstar1 ↦
> http://911research.wtc7.net/wtc/official/nist/NISTNCSTAR1Draft_text.html
• http://tinyurl.com/hoffmananamalies ↦
> http://911research.wtc7.net/sept11/analysis/anomalies.html
• http://tinyurl.com/shouldhavestood ↦ http://www.nowpublic.com/world/
> world-trade-center-building-designers-pre-9-11-claims-strongly-
> should-have-implicate-owers-remained-standing-9-11

p. 21 • http://tinyurl.com/WTCgoingup ↦
> http://911research.wtc7.net/mirrors/guardian2/wtc/eng-news-record.htm

p. 24 • http://tinyurl.com/NIST2005 ↦
> http://wtc.nist.gov/WTC_Conf_Sep13-15/session6/6McAllister2.pdf
• http://tinyurl.com/NIST2005finalRpt ↦
> http://wtc.nist.gov/NCSTAR1/PDF/NCSTAR%201.pdf

p. 25 • http://tinyurl.com/WTCdemolition ↦
> http://911research.wtc7.net/mirrors/guardian2/wtc/wtc-demolition.htm

p. 26 • http://tinyurl.com/massandpe ↦
> http://911research.wtc7.net/mirrors/guardian2/wtc/wtc-demolition.htm

p. 27 • http://tinyurl.com/symmetricalcollapse ↦
> .http://911research.wtc7.net/analysis/collapses/symmetry.html

p. 29 • http://tinyurl.com/casaliggi ↦ http://www.youtube.com/watch?v=eSueQsVsk_M

p. 30 • http://tinyurl.com/patakiwalk ↦
> http://www.youtube.com/watch?v=MDuBi8KyOhw

p. 31 • http://tinyurl.com/SouthTowermolten ↦
> http://www.youtube.com/watch?v=nbzdO0EPOGg
• http://tinyurl.com/astaneh ↦
> http://www.historycommons.org/entity.jsp?entity=abolhassan_astaneh_asl_1
• http://tinyurl.com/groundzeroanalysis ↦
> http://911research.wtc7.net/cache/wtc/analysis/asse_groundzero1.htm
• http://tinyurl.com/groundzerodangerous ↦
> http://www.osha.gov/Publications/WTC/dangerous_worksite.html

p. 32 • http://tinyurl.com/LeslieRobertson ↦
> http://www.youtube.com/watch?v=hLCwq3-RzZs
• http://tinyurl.com/moltenmetal ↦
> http://ae911truth.org/en/evidence.html#Videos_by_AE911Truth
• http://tinyurl.com/firefightertestimony ↦
> 911studies.com/articles/Article_5_118Witnesses_WorldTradeCenter.pdf

p. 33 • http://tinyurl.com/grosslies ↔
http://www.youtube.com/watch?v=fs_ogSbQFbM

• http://tinyurl.com/FEMAreport ↔
http://911research.wtc7.net/mirrors/fema_wtc/fema403_apc.pdf

• http://tinyurl.com/wpisteel ↔
http://www.wpi.edu/News/Transformations/2002Spring/steel.html

p. 34 • http://tinyurl.com/missingjolt ↔
http://www.journalof911studies.com/volume/2008/TheMissingJolt7.pdf

p. 35 • http://tinyurl.com/explosionreports ↔
http://911research.wtc7.net/wtc/evidence/oralhistories/explosions.html

p. 39 • http://tinyurl.com/WTCfires ↔
http://whatreallyhappened.com/WRHARTICLES/wtc_fires_911.html

• http://tinyurl.com/unignitedthermite ↔ http://911blogger. com/news/2011-02-
20/dr-steven-jones-911-science-and-society-now-youtube

p. 39 • http://tinyurl.com/thermitepaper ↔
http://www.benthamscience.com/open/tocpj/articles/V002/7TOCPJ.htm?
TOCPJ/2009/00000002/00000001/7TOCPJ.SGM

• http://tinyurl.com/jonesarticle ↔ http://www.journalof911studies.com/
volume/200704/JonesWTC911SciMethod.pdf

p. 40 • http://tinyurl.com/microspheres ↔ http://ae911truth.org/news/41-articles/
348-previously-molten-iron-spheres-were-in-wtc-dust-
reveal-use-of-thermitic-materials.html

• http://tinyurl.com/thermitepyrotechnics ↔
http://911research.wtc7.net/essays/thermite/thermitics_made_simple.html

• http://tinyurl.com/explosiveresidues ↔
http://911research.wtc7.net/essays/thermite/explosive_residues.html

• http://tinyurl.com/hightemperatures ↔
http://www.journal of911studies.com/articles/WTCHighTemp2.pdf

• http://tinyurl.com/RJLeereport ↔ http://911research.wtc7.net/essays/thermite/
cache/nyenvirolaw_WTCDustSignatureCompositionAndMorphology.pdf

• http://tinyurl.com/truthburningman ↔http://911truthburn.blogspot.com/
2007/05/truthburn-art-project-at-burning-man.html

p. 41 • http://tinyurl.com/WTCcleanup ↔ http://911research.wtc7.net/cache/wtc/
analysis/collapses/wasteage_cleanup.htm

p. 43 • http://tinyurl.com/appendixL ↔
http://wtc.nist.gov/progress_report_june04/appendixl.pdf

• http://tinyurl.com/sidebysidedemolitions ↔
http://www.youtube.com/watch?v=73qK4j32iuo

p. 44 • http://tinyurl.com/ganserarticle ↔
http://sc.tagesanzeiger.ch/dyn/news/ausland/663864.html

• http://tinyurl.com/griffinamemp ↔ http://www.journalof911studies.com/
volume/200704/DavidRayGriffin911Empire.pdf

• http://tinyurl.com/sundertalk ↔
http://911speakout.org/NIST_Tech_Briefing_Transcript.pdf

• http://tinyurl.com/NISTonfreefall ↔
http://www.nist.gov/public_affairs/factsheet/wtc_qa_082108.cfm

p. 45 • http://tinyurl.com/kevinmcpadden ↔
http://www.youtube.com/watch?v=STbD9XMCOho

p. 46 • http://tinyurl.com/janestandley ↔
http://www.youtube.com/watch?v=ltP2t9nq9fI

• http://tinyurl.com/shapiroarticle ↔
http://www.foxnews.com/opinion/2010/04/22/jeffrey-scott-shapiro
-jesse-venture-book-lies-truthers-ground-zero-sept-shame

• http://tinyurl.com/jonescomment ↔ http://www.prisonplanet.com/
bombshell-silverstein-wanted-to-demolish-building-7-on-911.html

p. 47 • http://tinyurl.com/aevideo ↔
http://ae911truth.org/en/evidence.html#Videos_by_AE911Truth

p. 48 • http://tinyurl.com/commission1 ↔
http://911research.wtc7.net/post911/commission/index.html
• http://tinyurl.com/commission2 ↔
http://911research.wtc7.net/post911/commission/report.html
• http://tinyurl.com/cameronstory ↔
http://www.foxnews.com/story/0,2933,53065,00.html
p. 49 • http://tinyurl.com/meacherarticle ↔
http://www.guardian.co.uk/politics/2003/sep/06/september11.iraq
p. 50 • http://tinyurl.com/ricequote ↔ http://articles.cnn.com/2004-04-08/politics/
rice.transcript_1_terrorist-threat-freedom-hating-terrorists-response-
across-several-administrations/6?_s=PM:ALLPOLITICS
• http://tinyurl.com/binladentranscript ↔ http://articles.cnn.com/2004-04-10/
politics/august6.memo_1_bin-conduct-terrorist-attacks-
abu-zubaydah?_s=PM:ALLPOLITICS
• http://tinyurl.com/911foreknowledge ↔ http://en.wikipedia.org/wiki
/September_11_attacks_advance-knowledge_debate (with 81 references)
p. 51 • http://tinyurl.com/brownwarned ↔
http://www.sfgate.com/today/0912_chron_mnreport.shtml
• http://tinyurl.com/Rushdieairban ↔
http://911research.wtc7.net/cache/sept11/londontimes_rushdieairban.htm
p. 52 • http://tinyurl.com/odigoworkers ↔ http://www.haaretz.com/
print-edition/news/odigo-says-workers-were-warned-of-attack-1.70579
• http://tinyurl.com/911putoptions ↔
http://www.cbsnews.com/stories/2001/09/19/eveningnews/main311834.shtml
• http://tinyurl.com/putoptions2 ↔
http://www.lionhrtpub.com/orms/orms-6-04/predict.html
• http://tinyurl.com/911commissionreport ↔ http://911research.wtc7.net/
mirrors/911commission/report/911Report_Notes.htm
p. 54 • http://tinyurl.com/hoffmananomalies ↔
http://911research.wtc7.net/sept11/analysis/anomalies.html
• http://tinyurl.com/hanihanjour ↔
http://911research.wtc7.net/disinfo/deceptions/badpilots.html
• http://tinyurl.com/hijackerstrained ↔ http://www.newsweek.com/2001
/09/14/alleged-hijackers-may-have-trained-at-u-s-bases.html
• http://tinyurl.com/resurrectedhijackers ↔
http://911research.wtc7.net/disinfo/deceptions/identities.html
p. 55 • http://tinyurl.com/hijackingcode ↔
http://www.time.com/time/nation/article/0,8599,174912,00.html
• http://tinyurl.com/hoffmananomalies ↔
http://911research.wtc7.net/sept11/analysis/anomalies.html
• http://tinyurl.com/carousingjihadists ↔
http://911research.wtc7.net/disinfo/deceptions/carousers.html
• http://tinyurl.com/carousers2 ↔
http://www.usatoday.com/news/nation/2001/09/14/miami-club.htm
• http://tinyurl.com/hoffmananomalies ↔
http://911research.wtc7.net/sept11/analysis/anomalies.html
• http://tinyurl.com/resurrectedhijackers ↔
http://911research.wtc7.net/disinfo/deceptions/identities.html
• http://tinyurl.com/novideos ↔
http://911research.wtc7.net/planes/evidence/airportvideo.html
p. 56 • http://tinyurl.com/hijackersalive ↔ http://news.bbc.co.uk/2/hi/1559151.stm
• http://tinyurl.com/fakeIDs ↔ http://archives.cnn.com/2001/US/09/21/inv.id.theft
• http://tinyurl.com/robertsessay ↔
http://911research.wtc7.net/essays/roberts/index.html
p. 57 • http://tinyurl.com/NORADstanddown ↔
http://911research.wtc7.net/planes/analysis/norad/index.html
p. 58 • http://tinyurl.com/Pentagonrenovation ↔
http://911research.wtc7.net/pentagon/renovation.html

p. 58 • http://tinyurl.com/ATCsrecall ↭
> http://911review.com/cache/errors/pentagon/abcnews102401b.html

• http://tinyurl.com/attackonPentagon ↭
> http://911research.wtc7.net/pentagon/attack/index.html

• http://tinyurl.com/hoffmananomalies ↭
> http://911research.wtc7.net/sept11/analysis/anomalies.html

• http://tinyurl.com/hanihanjour ↭
> http://911research.wtc7.net/disinfo/deceptions/badpilots.html

p. 59 • http://tinyurl.com/DODvideos ↭
> http://911research.wtc7.net/pentagon/evidence/videos/dodvideos.html

• http://tinyurl.com/noplanetheory ↭
> http://911research.wtc7.net/essays/pentagontrap.html

• http://tinyurl.com/missingevidence ↭
> http://911research.wtc7.net/pentagon/evidence/missing.html

p. 60 • http://tinyurl.com/93blackbox ↭ http://911research.wtc7.net/
> cache/planes/attack/cnn_blackboxfound.htmlp.

• http://tinyurl.com/93crashsite ↭
> http://911research.wtc7.net/planes/attack/flight93site.html

• http://tinyurl.com/crashof93 ↭
> http://911research.wtc7.net/planes/analysis/flight93/index.html

p. 62 • http://tinyurl.com/93witnesses ↭
> http://911research.wtc7.net/planes/evidence/flight93witnesses.html

• http://tinyurl.com/Bushon911 ↭
> http://www.historycommons.org/essay.jsp?article=essayaninterestingday

p. 63 • http://tinyurl.com/Bushcoverstories ↭
> http://911research.wtc7.net/disinfo/alibis/bush.html

• http://tinyurl.com/CNNBushtranscript ↭
> http://transcripts.cnn.com/TRANSCRIPTS/0112/04/se.04.html

p. 64 • http://tinyurl.com/bushreaction ↭ http://911research.wtc7.net/cache/
> disinfo/alibis/washingtontimes_timetolead.htm

p. 65 • http://tinyurl.com/Bushcoverstories ↭
> http://911research.wtc7.net/disinfo/alibis/bush.html

p. 66 • http://tinyurl.com/elevatorproject ↭
> http://911research.wtc7.net/cache/wtc/arch/wtc_elevator_renovation.pdf

p. 67 • http://tinyurl.com/wirtwalker ↭ http://911blogger.com/news/2010-09-03/
> history-wirt-dexter-walker-russell-company-cia-and-911

• http://tinyurl.com/WTCaccess ↭
> http://911review.com/articles/ryan/demolition_access_p2.html

p. 71 •http://tinyurl.com/OpGladio ↭
> http://en.wikipedia.org/wiki/Operation_Gladio (with 94 references)

• http://tinyurl.com/flyersliars ↭
> http://en.wikipedia.org/wiki/Wright_brothers (with 97 references)

p. 73 • http://tinyurl.com/silversteinpayout ↭
> http://911research.wtc7.net/cache/wtc/background/fox23news_billions.html

• http://tinyurl.com/WTCowners ↭
> http://911research.wtc7.net/wtc/background/owners.html

p. 74 • http://tinyurl.com/pnacpaper ↭
> http://www.newamericancentury.org/RebuildingAmericasDefenses.pdf

p. 75 • http://tinyurl.com/lengthofwars ↭ http://en.wikipedia.org/wiki/
> Length_of_U.S._participation_in_major_wars (with 22 references)

p. 78 • http://tinyurl.com/Northwds ↭
> http://en.wikipedia.org/wiki/Operation_Northwoods (with 21 references)

p. 89 • http://tinyurl.com/whitmanlied ↭ http://www.nydaily news.com/
> news/2007/12/11/2007-12-_christie_whitman

p. 91 • http://tinyurl.com/completetimeline ↭ http://www.historycommons.org/
> project.jsp?project=911_project

p. 92 • http://tinyurl.com/good911DVDs ↭
> http://911research.wtc7.net/resources/videos/index.html

• http://tinyurl.com/good911books ↭
> http://911research.wtc7.net/resources/books/books.html

Index